1957

From

Laura + Ralph

D1521155

# THE CHURCH'S TEACHING

## I
### The Holy Scriptures

## II
### Chapters in Church History

*In Preparation*

The Faith of the Church

The Worship of the Church

Christian Living

The Church at Work

# THE HOLY SCRIPTURES

# THE HOLY

## The Church's Teaching

**NEW YORK** • The National Coun

# CRIPTURES

. . . . . *Volume One*

*by* ROBERT C. DENTAN, Ph.D.

*with the assistance of the Authors'*
*Committee: Frederick Q. Shafer, John*
*Heuss, D.D., James A. Pike, J.S.D.,*
*C. Kilmer Myers, Vesper O. Ward,*
*Stanley Brown-Serman, D.D., Powel*
*M. Dawley, Ph.D., T. O. Wedel, Ph.D.*

Protestant Episcopal Church • 1951

*First Published December, 1949*
*Second Printing, January, 1950*
*Third Printing, February, 1950*
*Fourth Printing, April, 1950*
*Fifth Printing, October, 1950*
*Sixth Printing, February, 1951*

PRINTED IN THE UNITED STATES OF AMERICA

# ABOUT THE AUTHOR

THE REV. ROBERT CLAUDE DENTAN, PH.D., is Professor of the Literature and Interpretation of the Old Testament at the Berkeley Divinity School, New Haven, Conn. A graduate of Colorado College and Berkeley Divinity School, Dr. Dentan spent a year of study at the American School of Oriental Research in Jerusalem and received his Ph.D. from Yale University. He was formerly priest-in-charge of St. John's Church, Donora, Pa., and rector of St. John's Church, New Haven, Conn.

### ABOUT OTHER MEMBERS OF THE COMMITTEE OF AUTHORS

THE REV. POWEL MILLS DAWLEY, PH.D., is Professor of Ecclesiastical History at the General Theological Seminary. A graduate of Brown University and the Episcopal Theological School, Cambridge, Mass., he received his Ph.D. from Cambridge University, England. He is co-author of *The Religion of the Prayer Book.*

THE REV. STANLEY BROWN-SERMAN, S.T.D., is a Professor of New Testament Language and Literature at the Theological Seminary, Alexandria, Va. He attended Keble College, Oxford, and Columbia University. He is the co-author of *What Did Jesus Think?*

THE REV. JAMES ALBERT PIKE, J.S.D., is Chaplain of Columbia University in New York. A graduate of the University of Southern California, he was Sterling Fellow at the Yale Law School and received the degree of Doctor of Juridical Science there in 1938. For four years he was with the Office of the General Counsel, Securities and Exchange Commission in Washington, D. C., and has been lecturer in Civil and Federal Procedures at George Washington University School of Law. During World War II he served in the Navy. Dr. Pike, a former Roman Catholic, was ordained in 1944.

THE REV. THEODORE O. WEDEL, PH.D., is Warden of the College of Preachers in Washington, D. C. He is a graduate of Oberlin College and took his Ph.D. at Yale in 1918. He was Professor of English at Carleton College from 1922 to 1934; Secretary for College Work of the National Council, 1934 to 1939. He is the author of *The Coming Great Church.*

THE REV. C. KILMER MYERS is rector of Grace Church, Jersey City, N. J. A graduate of Rutgers University and Berkeley Divinity School, he has been an instructor in liturgics at Berkeley and General Theological Seminary. He is the author of *Liturgy and Life, The Church and the Seminary,* and *Unity through Liturgy.*

THE REV. FREDERICK Q. SHAFER is lecturer in religion at the University of the South in Sewanee, Tenn. He is a graduate of Bard College and the General Theological Seminary.

# CON

NTS

# *Foreword*

THIS book is one volume of a series called *The Church's Teaching,* prepared for use in the Episcopal Church. Other volumes in preparation include *Chapters in Church History, The Faith of the Church, The Worship of the Church, Christian Living,* and *The Church at Work.*

These books are written to provide adults with the basic content teaching of the Episcopal Church. They are not intended to be used as church school courses, although they can be a valuable resource in teaching children, youth, and adults.

These books are the joint production of the members of the Authors' Committee under the chairmanship of the Director of the Department of Christian Education of the National Council. They are the result of careful criticism and many months of writing and rewriting. What is here published represents the meeting of many minds.

This volume was read by a large group of scholars, clergymen, and laymen. A considerable majority agreed that the book is acceptable for the purpose for which it was written, and that it will be useful in acquainting readers with the general position of contemporary Biblical scholarship. The clergy and lay approval was enthusiastic to a degree which led to the decision to publish it in its present form.

For the coöperation of all who contributed in any way we are deeply grateful.

JOHN HEUSS

# PART ONE

# Introduction

# The Approach to the Bible

THE God in whom Christians believe is a God who has revealed Himself in history, and the Bible is the record of that revelation. The Bible is not primarily a book about men, but about God; its chief value is not that it contains great literature, but that it shows us what God is like and what God has done.

## THE BIBLE AS THE REVELATION OF GOD

THE God whom the Bible reveals is not an impersonal force, not a vague, remote Absolute whom we might call the Supreme Being, nor a mere law of nature, like the principle of gravitation. He is a personal God, One who loves, plans, creates, and reveals Himself. This does not mean that God has a physical body; nor does it mean that His will and emotions and plans are always changing like those of human personalities. No words used to describe human personality can have quite the same sense when applied to God. God is infinite and His personality is not changeable, as our limited human personalities are; His plans and purposes are eternal and His love is unchanging and unlimited. The God of the Bible is personal because persons, beings who can think, will, create, and love, are the highest things we know in all creation, and God must be at least as great as the greatest things which He has made. His nature must somehow include all those qualities which go to make human personality the noblest and most valuable thing we know.

It is important to understand this clearly because God Himself is the principal character in the Bible story, and all through the Bible He is revealed as acting like a person. He is not abstract and shadowy, but a living God who thinks, speaks, and acts. He made the world by the decree of His Will and has a plan for that world and has revealed His plan to His creatures. The Bible pictures the personal activity of God so vividly that it often seems to make Him act exactly as human beings do. It sometimes speaks of Him as having arms and hands and fingers. It even speaks of God repenting of what He has done. Such expressions are not to be taken literally, but are simply vivid ways of making us realize that God is intensely real and that our relationship with Him is not with some ill-defined idea in our own minds nor with some force of nature, but is the relationship of persons with a Person. The God of the Bible is not an It to be impersonally discussed; He is a Thou, who at every point confronts us with an invitation to believe and a command to obey.[1]

---

[1] The Christian doctrine of God is discussed at greater length in another volume of this series.

## HOW GOD REVEALS HIMSELF

BECAUSE God is personal and has made us "in His image" *(Genesis 1:26)* to be His children, He desires to reveal Himself to us in order that we may know and love Him. For those whose minds and hearts are prepared to receive it, the revelation of God is unmistakable. It takes place in three general ways.

First of all, God reveals Himself in *Nature,* not because Nature is the same thing as God, but because God created and controls it. From Nature one can learn that God exists, and, since Nature was created by God, it shows something of the character of its Creator. In the beauty and orderliness and dependability of the natural world we can see reflected the beauty and order and dependability of God.

In the second place, God reveals Himself in certain great acts in *History.* As Christians, we are chiefly concerned with this revelation, since it is the belief that God has manifested Himself in history which distinguishes the Christian and Jewish religions from most other religions.

In the third place, God reveals Himself through the inspired insights of great men whom we call *Prophets.* This is really just another side of God's revelation in history, because we should not understand the meaning of sacred history if there were no one capable of explaining it. Ordinary men look at the events of history and see in them only the operation of chance or of mechanistic laws; the prophet looks at these same events and sees in them the unfolding of God's eternal purpose. The prophet speaks, of course, primarily, to his own contemporaries, but because he deals with eternal things his message has

7

enduring significance. It is because of the great prophetic personalities of the Old and New Testaments that we are able today to understand the meaning of the story which the Bible tells. It should be understood, of course, that the word prophet used in this sense is not limited to those who are technically called prophets; it includes all great religious teachers who help men better to understand the wonderful works of God.

## GOD'S SPECIAL REVELATION IN THE BIBLE

IN some sense, no doubt, God reveals Himself in all history, but the Bible is the story of a particular section of history in which God chose to make Himself known in an unmistakable way. This is the history of Israel: the Old Israel of the Hebrew nation and the New Israel of the Christian Church. In this history, we see how God chose one nation to be the agent of His revelation to all men everywhere. We see how God made Himself known to this nation by redeeming them out of the land of Egypt; how He guided and moulded them through the centuries that followed; and finally, how He finished His work of revelation by another great redeeming act, the victory of Christ over sin and death, and created the Church to proclaim the Good News to all humanity.

In the Bible we see God actually at work, creating, guiding, and redeeming. When we read the Bible, it is not as though we were in the classroom, listening to one teacher after another tell us things about God. It is rather as though we were in a theater and were seeing God engaged in the performance of His mighty acts. The drama of the redemption of mankind is a long and magnificent

8

one and the various chapters of Biblical history are the acts of the play. We must always remember that, even though we call it a drama, it is a drama that really happened. In all essential details, the history which is told in the Bible is true history.

### THE BIBLE AS THE WORD OF GOD

SINCE the Bible is the record of how God revealed Himself to mankind, it is properly called the Word of God. This is clear when we understand that here Word simply means communication or message. When we want to communicate our thoughts to others, we make use of words to do so. Sometimes we use the expression "word" in the singular to mean a sentence or a whole message, as when we say, "His last word to me was such and such," meaning someone's last connected thoughts. It is in this sense that the Bible is God's Word to man. In the Bible, we find God's own message about Himself. The Bible story contains that communication of the truth about Himself and about His purposes for the world which God desired mankind to have.

It is important to notice that when we say the Bible is the Word of God, we do not mean that it is so many different words of God, as though every separate word or verse, taken by itself, had God for its author. There is much in the Bible which clearly refers only to particular times or situations in the past. There is much that was true and valid for certain stages in the development of man's understanding, but is no longer valid once men have passed beyond that stage. There is much that is included in the Bible only because it helps us to understand the progress of the story. Some passages of Scripture are hard to interpret and some even offend our sense of Christian morality. But we are not intended to read the Bible in piecemeal fashion, interpreting every verse and chapter by itself. Many serious doctrinal and moral errors have arisen because people have drawn far-reaching conclusions from particular chapters or verses of the Bible without trying to see how that particular fragment fits into the larger pattern. The particular words must be seen in the light of the Word as a whole.

From the Bible story as a whole we learn: what God is like; whence man came; what God intended man to be; how man, by rejecting God's plan and choosing his own, has brought himself to his present tragic state; and how God Himself has provided the means of release which make it possible for men to realize the glorious destiny of divine sonship for which they were created. This story, in all its sweep and grandeur, is God's Word to man.

## THE INSPIRATION OF THE BIBLE

EVERYONE would agree that the Bible is an inspired book, but not all would agree as to what inspired means. In common speech, the word is often used in quite loose fashion to mean something that is extraordinarily fine, as when we say that Shakespeare is an inspired poet. Some would explain the doctrine of the inspiration of the Bible as nothing more than an extension of this use of the term. The Bible, they would say, is inspired in the same sense in which all great literature is inspired, only more so. When the Church, however, uses the term she means something much more than this. She means that, in some quite definite and unique way, the Bible is the work of God the Holy Spirit.

The Bible is inspired, first of all, because it has an inspired story to tell. It is a unique story which is not just the history of a particular nation or an interesting group of people, but a story in which God is the principal actor. Behind the whole great drama with its colorful events and its richly human characters, we see God directing its course and shaping the end toward which it moves.

But it is also the Church's faith that God, who presides over the story, presided also in some way over the writing down of the story, so that the essential meaning was not distorted by human misunderstanding and thus lost to future generations. God the Holy Spirit has watched over the growth and preservation of this book so that we can trust it as a reliable record of what God has done for us, and can accept its general view of the world as a dependable basis for our own faith and conduct.

This does not mean that we are bound to believe that every single word and verse in the Bible has been dictated by God and is therefore unfailingly true (the doctrine commonly called *verbal infallibility*). There are many things in the Bible which would make it difficult to hold this view: contradictions, incidental errors of fact, and ideas which are clearly of human origin. More important than these considerations, however, is the fact that such a view would make the Bible an unreal, almost magical book, and would seem to represent God as acting in a way which is unlike the way in which He works elsewhere.

In the Bible story, we find God always working through men, real, human, fallible men like ourselves. The great characters of the Biblical drama are warm, human, and lovable. The Bible never hesitates to show their faults as well as their virtues. Even in the stupendous event of the Incarnation, which is the central event of Scripture and of all history, God did not choose to reveal Himself through a demigod, one far removed from our common humanity, but through One who was perfectly Man, "in all things . . . made like unto his brethren" *(Hebrews 2:17)*. So when God gave us the Bible and made use of human beings as its authors, we should not expect that He would take away their natural human qualities from them: their special interests, their own style of writing, even their capacity to make mistakes. God did not overpower their minds and hands so that they ceased to be creative writers and became, instead, merely His secretaries. The work of inspiration was rather that of a gentle influence which guided their work as a whole and made sure that the total picture was not false or distorted and that nothing essential was omitted.

### THE UNITY OF THE BIBLE

THE Bible is divided into two parts, the Old and the New Testaments, and each part is essential for the Christian Faith. Sometimes one part has been overemphasized at the expense of the other. Some of our religious ancestors were inclined to depend too much upon the Old Testament and to slight the distinctive teaching of the New. Today, we are tempted to do the opposite and think of the Old Testament as merely a Jewish book which is not really necessary for Christians. There are those who set the Old Testament against the New as though it taught a dreadful kind of religion from which we have now been happily delivered. This is not the teaching of the New Testament itself nor has such a view ever been accepted by the Church.

According to the Christian view, the Bible is a single, organic whole which, though it is composed of many books by many authors, has a single story to tell. It is like a play in two great acts, neither of which can be understood without the other. If one read the Old Testament without going on to the New, he would miss the climax of the drama and the point of the whole story, since the New Testament contains the necessary conclusion of the story which the Old Testament starts out to tell. On the other hand, to read the New Testament without the Old would be like trying to understand the last chapter of a long novel without bothering to read the earlier part of the book, which sets the scene, introduces the characters, and describes the basic conflicts which are to be resolved.

## THE BACKGROUND OF OLD TESTAMENT HISTORY

SINCE the chief danger today is a neglect of the Old Testament, it is necessary to set forth in somewhat fuller detail the reasons for including it among the things about which a Christian should know "to his soul's health." There are two directions in which an understanding of the Old Testament is especially required for an understanding of the New.

First of all one must know the general outline of Old Testament history in order to understand the historical situation which is pictured in the New Testament, and the allusions to that history which the New Testament writers make on nearly every page. Just as one could not hope to understand the American people without knowing in general what their history has been from the founding of the colonies down to the present, so one cannot hope to understand the Jews, from among whom Jesus came and to whom He addressed His message, unless one has some knowledge of the long history which formed their character and created their peculiar problems. From one point of view, the events related in the New Testament may really be considered the last chapters in the heroic story of ancient Israel. These events are the high point of that story: the one great goal toward which it had really been moving from the very first.

If we look at the Gospel of St. Matthew, we discover a striking example of this in the very first chapter. More than half the chapter is merely a list of names taken from the Old Testament, names which would be meaningless to a person unfamiliar with Old Testament history. It seems a dull way to begin a book, but the writer evidently felt that it was necessary right at the outset to show Jesus Christ in His proper place as the end and fulfilment of the whole long history which had gone before.

The other New Testament writers had a similar point of view. There is hardly a page of the New Testament that does not have something to say about the men or events of the Old. The Old Testament was the sacred book of Jesus and Paul and the other men of New Testament times, the only Bible they knew. They constantly make casual references to Abraham, Moses, David, and the prophets and do not trouble to explain these things in detail, because they rightly assumed that the people to whom they were speaking already had a thorough knowledge of the Old Testament story. For this reason, if for no other, we can hardly hope to understand their message unless we also know that story.

In addition to the general background of Old Testament history which the New Testament assumes that we know, there is also a great background of concepts, ideas, and attitudes with which the New Testament writers take it for granted that we are familiar. There are many subjects on which the New Testament has little to say, not because it is indifferent to them, but because it assumes that Christians already will be thoroughly acquainted with the thought of the Old Testament and will have absorbed such ideas there.

In the New Testament, for example, there is surprisingly little of what is called the doctrine of God. The New Testament assumes that the Christian will know what God is like from reading the Old Testament. There he will learn:

that God is personal
that He is the Creator
that He loves the world which He has created
that He has a plan for mankind
that He rules over the forces of history
that He demands justice and brotherhood among His children
that He punishes wickedness and rewards goodness
that He is a God who saves and redeems.

All these things must first be understood before we can

understand the special features which the New Testament has to add to that general picture.

Even what is often regarded as the most characteristic New Testament idea about God, that He is a Father, is rooted in the Old Testament and is clearly suggested in the teaching of such prophets as Hosea, Jeremiah, and Malachi. What is remarkable in the New Testament is not the doctrine itself, but the new emphasis which is placed upon it.

To take another example, the New Testament has little to say about God's demands for justice and brotherhood in social relationships. This does not mean that the New Testament writers were not interested in such things, but that they took it for granted that their readers were already familiar with the pronouncements of the Hebrew prophets on this subject.

One of the later chapters of this book, Religious Faith and Practice in the Old Testament (pages 100-116), describes the most important of these Old Testament ideas which the New Testament presupposes and without which the New Testament cannot really be understood.

NEW TESTAMENT ESSENTIAL TO UNDERSTANDING OLD

JUST as the Old Testament is necessary for understanding the New, so, for Christians, the New Testament gives the necessary key for understanding the Old. When one comes to the end of any story, things which were said or done in earlier episodes take on a depth of meaning which they did not have when the reader first encountered them. When one reads through any book a second time, if the book is worth reading, one sees an inner relationship between seemingly disconnected events and subtle shades of meaning in speeches made by the characters which ·one did not see at first reading. The story has a new logic and the meaning of particular events is illuminated by the new-found logic of the whole. When we, as Christians, use the Old Testament in our worship and in our meditation, there is hardly a passage in it which does not take on some new meaning because we know that God's perfect revelation in Christ is the end of the story. The great poetry of the Psalms, the work of the prophets, the tales told of the heroes of Israel, the ethical ideals of Israel's teachers, all receive a new illumination when seen in the light of Christian experience. The Christian can never be content merely to interpret the Old Testament in the light of the times in which it was written. For him, it is a Christian book and its true significance is disclosed only when it is bound up in a single volume with the New Testament and interpreted in the light of the final and perfect revealing act of God which the New Testament describes. This inner and essential relationship between the two Testaments is what we mean by the unity of Bible.

## THE OLD TESTAMENT: PREPARATION FOR THE GOSPEL

THE Old Testament may be defined, from a purely human and objective point of view, as the literature of ancient Israel. In one of the popular editions of the classics, the volumes containing the Old Testament are called Ancient Hebrew Literature. But even from this standpoint it differs from other collections of literature coming down from antiquity, since Israel was different from all other ancient peoples. The ancient Hebrews had a concern for God which sets them apart from the rest of the ancient world and their literature is marked by an almost exclusive preoccupation with religious ideas and behavior.

For Christian believers, this complete absorption of the writers of Israel in God and in His plan for man is something more than national or racial genius. It is evidence of the election (that is, the Divine Choice) of Israel to fulfil a high and unique destiny. When God began the great work of redeeming His Creation He chose for Himself, as the Bible says, "a peculiar people" who were to be His servants and messengers. However, as with any servants, there had to be a period of preparation, and the Old Testament is the story of this preparatory stage.

There were certain attitudes which the people of Israel had to acquire; certain ideas of God and Man which had to be deeply impressed upon them. Perhaps most important of all, they had to learn the profound meaning of human sin and man's inability to realize his great possibilities and to attain his deepest desires by his own efforts. So Old Testament history is largely the story of a deepening sense of national frustration and tragedy. Through the teaching of the great prophets the people of Israel were brought to understand the meaning of their own, and of all, tragedy. The spiritual leaders of the nation were brought to a point where they realized that the hope of man was not in himself, but in God. They came really to understand that, apart from God's willingness to aid and lift him out of the mire in which he is sunk, man's cause is hopeless.

The people of Israel were reminded constantly that God once had saved them out of the dark bondage of Egypt. Later they experienced a similar deliverance from the Babylonian exile. Those who understood the meaning of these things could never really doubt either God's power or His willingness to save. What God had done in the past, they were sure He would do again. So the Old Testament closes in a mood of eager expectation, a belief that God would soon intervene once more to save His people *(Isaiah 60:1-3; Malachi 3:1)*. There were some even who saw that what was needed was not merely deliverance from external bondage, but from sin, which was the real root of their trouble *(Psalm 130:8; Isaiah 53:4-5)*. This new great act of God, they believed, would be the last, for by it God would establish His eternal Kingdom *(Daniel 7:27)*.

The New Testament begins just where the Old Testament leaves off. In the first chapter of the Gospel of St. Mark, the first of the gospels to be written, it says, *Jesus came into Galilee, preaching the gospel of the kingdom of God and saying, "The time is fulfilled, and the kingdom of God is at hand."* The Old Testament looks forward to a redemption yet to come; the New Testament looks back on a redemption already accomplished.

The Old Testament, then, is the story of the first long stage in the history of Israel, the people of God. In its first stage, Israel was a nation and membership in it was determined chiefly by the accident of birth. This was the only kind of spiritual community which could have been established under the conditions of the ancient Semitic world. With the beginning of the New Testament period, however, the old, national Israel had fulfilled its mission. Humanity was ready for a great new, creative movement in the drama of redemption. This did not mean that Israel was eliminated or that the idea of a holy nation was no longer important. It was still God's purpose to do His work through a spiritual community, a society, a brotherhood, which should be everywhere in the world, yet not of the world; a leaven which should gradually permeate the life of humanity. So out of the Old Israel and continuous with it, there grew the New Israel, the Christian Church. This body was no longer restricted in membership by requirements of race and nation, but was freely open to all: to Greek and Jew, to barbarian and Scythian, to slave and free citizen *(Colossians 3:11)*.

In the New Testament and the history of the Church we continue to read the history of Israel, for the idea of the Church as the New Israel is basic to any understanding of what the Church claims to be. The Old Testament is not, therefore, just the history of some curious, ancient people who somehow provided the historical and physical environment in which our Lord and his apostles worked. It is our own history, the first chapter in the story of that great spiritual and redemptive movement which began with the Exodus from Egypt and which continues to the present day. We are a part of that movement.

## THE APOCRYPHA: A NECESSARY LINK

BETWEEN the Old and New Testaments, many Bibles do, and all Bibles should, contain a section called The Apocrypha. These are books which appear only in the Greek version of the Old Testament, the Septuagint, and not in the

Hebrew. They, therefore, were regarded by the Jews of Palestine as of inferior worth and not treated as a part of Holy Scripture.

The Christian Church has not been entirely agreed as to what the status of these books should be. Some, notably the Roman Catholics, regard them as fully canonical, while others reject them entirely. The position of the Episcopal Church (as expressed in the sixth of the Articles of Religion) is that they are good and useful books, which ought to be read, but which are not to be used to prove any point of doctrine. This is certainly a sane and reasonable point of view. While none of these books reaches the heights which the Old Testament reaches at its greatest, yet the Apocrypha contains fascinating and sometimes inspiring stories like those of Tobit and Judith, excellent moral and ethical literature such as Ecclesiasticus, significant theological literature like the Wisdom of Solomon, and important history such as First Maccabees. The Apocryphal literature is extremely important for helping to understand the historical and religious developments which took place between the Testaments.

**THE NEW TESTAMENT: PROCLAMATION OF THE GOSPEL**

LIKE the Old Testament, the New is a collection of writings of different types and of different degrees of interest and value. It is not a systematic treatise on Christian doctrine. It is a very much smaller book and less complex than the Old Testament; it covers a much smaller period of time, and contains a smaller variety of literary types.

Its books fall into four divisions: accounts of the life of Jesus (the Gospels), the early history of the apostolic

21

Church (Acts), letters of St. Paul and other great figures of the apostolic age (the Epistles), and an apocalypse (Revelation). These books were not written originally with the intention of making them part of a new Christian scripture, since the Christian Church already had what it considered a sufficient scripture in the Old Testament. They were intended to meet the needs of particular times and places such, for example, as:

The need to preserve in written form the life and teachings of Jesus when the age of the eye-witnesses began to draw to a close.

The need to deal with situations which arose in the new churches which had been founded in Galatia, Corinth, Colossae, etc.

The need to give some guidance for the crisis created by the beginning of persecution.

These writings were all intended for specific situations and can be understood properly only if those situations are kept in mind.

In the early ages of the Church, there were many such writings, but with the rise of heresy (false and dangerous beliefs), it became necessary to make a selection among them to safeguard the faith. The books now included in the New Testament were finally recognized by general agreement within the Church as safe and trustworthy accounts of the faith of Christian believers during the first generation. In this way, the Church eventually developed a body of Christian scriptures roughly parallel to the older scriptures. They were given the name New Testament since they describe the means by which God's New Covenant was established, and the way in which it was understood by the generation which stood closest to the events.

The books of the New Testament were written under the over-ruling influence of God's Holy Spirit and provide a reliable standard for Christian belief and practice. Once again it must be emphasized that we are not to interpret individual passages by themselves, torn out of their context, nor may we just select certain passages we like and ignore others. That which is important in the New Testament is not the beauty or historical accuracy of certain particular verses or chapters, but the whole faith to which the whole New Testament bears witness.

Underlying all the obvious differences in point of view in the different books, the New Testament bears unified witness to one great fact, that God the Son has completed the great work of revelation and redemption, and that men are saved only as they joyfully accept what God has done. This message is called the Gospel (Good News). While there always will be considerable discussion as to the value of this or that particular passage, or the historical factuality of some particular incident, there can be no doubt as to the nature of the faith which the whole New Testament affirms, nor need there be any doubt as to the correctness in all essential matters of the story which it tells.

### THE DEVOTIONAL USE OF THE BIBLE

As we turn from considering these basic facts about the Bible and begin to study the Bible itself, it is important to remember that it is not merely a source of sacred history and of inspired ideas, for this would make it just a record of God's revelation in the past. This might lead us to think that the Word of God is a dead thing, something once spoken but now preserved in fossil form within the covers of a book. But God's Word is a living Word and Christian people have always believed that God makes use of the Bible to speak directly to the heart and conscience of the individual in every age. The Bible is a sacramental thing by means of which God gives His Word to everyone who comes to it in a spirit of prayer and humility. For the Christian it is never enough to read the Bible as great literature or even as the record of dramatic and significant events of the past. He must also read the Bible in a devotional way, asking for the guidance of God's Holy Spirit and expecting that, from time to time, he will hear God speaking from its pages in words clearly addressed to his own needs. When we read the Bible in this fashion, it takes on a new meaning. It becomes a living, present-day revelation: God's word to us.

*Prepare Ye
the Way
of the Lord*

## PART TWO

# The Old Testament

# Historical Books: *I. How Israel Became a Nation*

THE Old Testament is a library rather than a book. It consists of thirty-nine books representing a great variety of literary types. In English Bibles, these are arranged in three main divisions: History (Genesis-Esther), Poetry (Job-Song of Solomon) and Prophecy (Isaiah-Malachi). It is convenient to study the contents of the books under these headings, although we should remember that the division is somewhat artificial and does not correspond to that of the Hebrew Bible, which arranges them in a different order under the three headings: Law, Prophets, and Writings.

It is also important to remember that only a very few of the smaller books of the Old Testament came into existence in the fashion of modern books. Most of them are not the work of an individual author who sat down and wrote the entire book in the space of a few weeks or months. They are, rather, the result of a long process of growth and accumulation and have come to their present form through the work of several successive generations of editors. Practically speaking, they are all anonymous. Even those books which have the name of a particular person attached to them are so-called simply for convenience, sometimes because that person was one of the principal actors in the story (*e.g.* Samuel or Ezra), sometimes because his work was the nucleus around which the book grew (*e.g.* Isaiah), sometimes because tradition liked to attribute certain classes of writing to certain great men of the past (*e.g.* Proverbs to Solomon; Psalms to David).

### THE NATURE OF THE HISTORICAL BOOKS

THE historical books in their present form were composed by editors who lived in the sixth century B.C. or later. They used ancient documents and fragments which had been handed down to them as a part of the precious traditions of the nation and wove them into a single straight-forward narrative. Since they were anxious to use as much as possible of this old tradition, they did not hesitate to include even different accounts of the same event. Thus we frequently discover the strange fact that a single story will be told more than once. It is this which explains the contradictions and inconsistencies which occasionally occur in the Bible story. The editors could easily have removed these if they had desired to do so, but they had a great reverence for the material in its original form and preferred to let the older documents speak for themselves, even though their witness was sometimes a bit confusing. We are grateful for this habit of the Hebrew historians, because it means that when we read the books of the Old

Testament, we are not simply seeing ancient history as it appeared to the men of the sixth century, but actually have before us the oldest historical records of the Hebrew people. By using a certain amount of ingenuity, it is possible to separate out the various materials which the editors have used and thus to study directly these old and very exciting documents.

The first five books of the Old Testament stand in a special class and are called collectively the Pentateuch, meaning the Five Books. These are the books which the Jews called the Law and regarded as the most sacred part of the Bible. They tell the story of the Hebrew people down through the giving of the Law to Moses upon Mount Sinai and the approach of the children of Israel to the borders of the Promised Land. Scholars have succeeded in discovering at least four different older documents which were woven together to form these books and call them by the somewhat mysterious symbols J, E, D, and P.[1] We shall not be much concerned with these in our present discussion, but the reader should at least realize when he comes across these symbols, that they actually stand for four originally independent books now fused into one consecutive story. In the English Bible the books of the Pentateuch are all called Books of Moses, but the tradition that Moses wrote them is a comparatively late one and the books themselves make no such claim. Moses is the hero rather than the author, and does indeed occupy the center

---

[1] The oldest of these documents (about 850 B.C.), J, is so called because it prefers the name Jehovah or Jahweh (also spelt Yahweh) for God; the E document (about 750 B.C.) prefers the name Elohim (simply God in English). D stands for Deuteronomy (621 B.C.) and P for the priestly document, the latest of them all.

of the stage from the beginning of the book of Exodus through Deuteronomy.

## HOW THE WORLD BEGAN

IT is proper that the whole Bible should begin with a book called Genesis since the word *genesis* means beginning and this is the book which contains the ancient Hebrew stories about the beginnings of everything: the physical world, men, nations, languages, sin, suffering, and death. It is not a book of science, but a book of religion. We do not turn to it to learn what we can learn much better from scientific textbooks on geology or biology. The account of the origin of things which we find in this book is simply what the ancient Hebrews believed to be true according to the best knowledge of their time. The things with which Genesis has to do are really all things which took place long before real history existed and the stories are for the most part simply traditional tales which are not to be understood as reports of things that actually happened just so. That which is of permanent significance in this book is not its science or its history, but the amazing religious insights which it shows. No other people in the world have produced a book which can compare with this in its view of the meaning of human life. Although it is written for the most part in prose, it is, in a real sense, a book of poetry, a great epic of creation, and, in order to understand it, we must approach it from a poetic and imaginative point of view.

At the head of the book stand the solemn words *In the beginning God created the heaven and the earth,* and these words sum up the religious meaning of the whole account of the physical creation which follows. To whatever conclusion science may come in any age as to how the physical universe began and how man arose within it (and we must never forget that what we regard as scientific fact today may well be regarded as ignorant superstition tomorrow), the Bible still contains the most basic of all truths, that God stands back of the entire process. The world did not come into existence by mere chance and accident, but is the creation of an eternal and all powerful Mind, who had a purpose to fulfil.

The story which follows these words in the first chapter of Genesis is a magnificent imaginative description of the way in which God created the ordered Universe, gradually bringing order out of chaos by impressing His mind and will upon it. God is above the process and accomplishes it merely by speaking His word, which is the Hebrew way of saying that He did it by His thought. The events which this chapter describes happened long before the remotest beginnings of human history and, of course, can actually neither be described nor understood, but nowhere else will one find a picture of the creative process which gives such a real sense of its meaning and its wonder.

## HOW MAN WAS CREATED AND HOW HE FELL

THE climax of the creation story is the creation of *man*, in God's "image and likeness." There we see a second great spiritual truth: the sanctity of the human personality. Later on in the book, we are told that this is the reason for the prohibition of murder *(Genesis 9:6)*. One must not kill his brother man because every man, whether small or great, has something Godlike about him. This conception lies at the root of the distinctively Christian belief in the absolute value of the individual human personality and is therefore the foundation of the whole Christian system of social ethics and morality.

When we read the first chapters of Genesis with an open mind, we discover a curious fact. There are two accounts of the creation of man, one in chapter 1 and another in chapter 2. This is due to the previously mentioned circumstance that the final editors of the book wove their story out of several older books and often let different accounts of the same event stand side by side without attempting to make them agree with each other. The story in chapter 1 is from what is called the P document, which is the latest of all, while the story in chapter 2 is from J, which was the earliest of all.

When one reads the stories and compares them with each other, it will be seen very quickly that the story in chapter 2 is a much more primitive story than that in chapter 1, since it describes God as creating man by moulding him with His hands out of clay rather than simply pronouncing the word or conceiving the idea. This second story, however, also has its spiritual meaning which no doubt led the editors to retain it. This story goes on to tell how man, after he was created, rebelled against God and thereby brought unhappiness and suffering into a world which God had intended to be wholly good. The story of Adam and Eve is a profound account of the psychology of man and states the inescapable truth that the sense of frustration which we often feel in our lives and in the lives of others around us has its origin in sin, and that sin, at its roots, is simply pride, our proud unwillingness to follow the plan of life which God has laid out for us. Because Adam and Eve chose to do what they wanted to do rather than what God wanted them to do, they were driven out of the garden where all was happy and peaceful into a world of heart-breaking toil and bitter struggle *(Genesis 3:17-19)*. It is worth noticing that the word Adam is simply the common Hebrew word for man. This gives us the clue for a proper understanding of the tale, which is really the story of Everyman.

The same ancient document, J, continues in chapter 4 with the story of Cain and Abel. People often ask foolish questions about this story, such as "Where did Cain get his wife?" because they do not understand that the people who preserved the story for us were not themselves interested in such merely factual matters. They told the story because they had it ready to hand and found in it an excellent parable of the growing sinfulness and cruelty of humankind. As soon as man sets himself up against God and cuts himself off from fellowship with God, then his lower nature takes possession of him and he begins to live on a purely selfish and brutal level, as expressed in the cynical phrase, *Am I my brother's keeper? (Genesis 4:9)*. The rest of the chapter leads up to the brief account of the unlimited violence of Lamech, who illustrates human nature at its unbridled worst *(Genesis 4:23, 24)*.

### THE FLOOD

BOTH ancient documents, J and P, proceed to tell the story of the Flood, an ancient and striking tale, which shows God's attitude toward sin *(Genesis 6-8)*. God is a God of purity and justice, and, when Man has utterly *corrupted his way upon earth (Genesis 6:12),* God passes judgment upon him and destroys him. The story is a dramatic parable illustrating the universal principle that God is *of purer eyes than to behold evil (Habakkuk 1:13)* and that every system of human life which is based upon injustice, violence, and bloodshed is bound to perish. It goes on to show, however, that the mere punishment of evil is never God's ultimate purpose. It is God's will that man be saved and eventually restored to perfect fellowship with Him. So out of the catastrophe which overwhelmed a sinful world, God saved the one righteous man whom He could find, Noah, and his family, with the purpose of beginning anew with the human family and salvaging something from the shipwreck which man had made of his own existence.

Once again, in the story of the descendants of Noah *(Genesis 10),* we see how the Old Testament conceived of the unity of the human race, for, as all men, of every race and nation, are descendants of the same first ancestor, so all are descendants of Noah by his three sons, Shem, Ham, and Japheth. God made a covenant, or agreement, with Noah, described in Genesis 9, which was to be binding on all his descendants. This is the Old Testament way of saying there is a universal moral law which must be obeyed by all men and which must be observed toward all men. The most important provision in this Noachite covenant is the demand to respect the sanctity of human life, for men, all men, are made in the image of God *(Genesis 9:6).* Thus we see at the very beginning of the Old Testament story how the purpose of God and His fatherly care extend to all the human race.

AFTER telling, in the story of the Tower of Babel, how man, by his foolish arrogance, again brought disunity and confusion into the world, the ancient epic then goes on to relate how God determined to save mankind by choosing a particular human family to be the agents of His revelation and redeeming work. God chose Abraham in the distant land of Mesopotamia and called upon him to leave his kindred and go to a new land of which he knew nothing except that God would give it to him *(Genesis 12)*. So Abraham, who lived in Haran (although his father is said to have come originally from Ur of the Chaldees) left his home and, accepting God's promise with perfect faith, crossed the desert with his dependents to settle in Canaan, the land which today we call Palestine. God promised that this land would be his and that all the families of the earth would be blessed in him *(Genesis 12:3)*. This agreement which God made with Abraham was the second of His great covenants with men, this time made not with the whole human race, but with one particular human family. The sign of this covenant was to be the rite of circumcision *(Genesis 17:1-14)*.

After they came to Canaan, Abraham separated from Lot his nephew, because their flocks and possessions were too large to permit them to dwell together, and Lot selfishly chose for himself the most beautiful part of the land, the fertile Jordan valley, where the great Canaanite cities of Sodom and Gomorrah were located *(Genesis 13)*. Afterwards, Abraham began to worry because he had no son to inherit his property, and Sarah, his wife, seemed too old to have children. He and Sarah, therefore, made an arrangement by which he took Sarah's serving maid, Hagar, as a kind of secondary wife, and she bore him a son whom they called Ishmael *(Genesis 16)*. All this was quite proper according to the laws which governed the nations of the Near East in those days. Sarah, however, was unhappy about the situation and, when God took pity upon her and gave her a son also, she drove Hagar and Ishmael from the house *(Genesis 16 and 21)*. It is a tragic story, but to the people of that ancient time Sarah would have seemed quite justified in attempting, at all costs, to protect the interests of her own child. This story is a good illustration of the fact that we must not take Old Testament moral standards as necessarily our own, although we should also be fair enough to recognize that in later times, even in Israel itself, the conduct of Sarah would certainly have been frowned upon. To the people who told the story, however, the important thing was that Abraham now had a son, whom he named Isaac, and that he was now assured that God's promise would be fulfilled. Abraham would have a family and that family, the Hebrew nation, would be a blessing to the whole world.

The story of Sodom and Gomorrah *(Genesis 18, 19)* illustrates once again God's hatred of evil, for the inhabitants of these cities, who belonged to the Canaanite race which inhabited the land when Abraham came, were completely corrupted by the perverseness of their sexual life and we are told that God at last destroyed them by a hail of fire and brimstone. The only persons saved from these cities were Lot and the members of his household. Lot was saved, not only because he was a member of Abraham's family, but because he was clearly a righteous man, who had a sense of decency and honor which his Canaanite neighbors did not possess. Knowledge which has come to us from the study of archaeology makes us realize that the picture here is essentially correct, for the Canaanites were a people of decadent morality and their general standard of conduct was far lower than that of the Hebrews. The final victory of the Hebrews over the Canaanites was due not simply to God's favoritism toward His own people, but to the inevitable victory of a virile people of high morality over a people whose morals were debased.

The most touching of all the stories about Abraham is the one which tells of his willingness to sacrifice to God even his only son Isaac, whom he loved more dearly than any other worldly possession (Genesis 22). Of course, we realize today that even the suggestion of human sacrifice is offensive to God, but in those remote days people were not quite sure. The most important thing about the story is that it represents God as merely putting Abraham to the test, with no thought of ever allowing him to carry it out. Abraham comes through the test completely vindicated and once more proves himself to be the great example of perfect faith in God. The story also expresses the conviction of the Hebrew people that God does not desire human sacrifice; a tremendous advance in man's conception of God.

### JACOB

GENESIS then goes on to tell the beautiful story of the betrothal and marriage of Isaac to Rebekah, a wife who belonged to a branch of his mother's clan which still remained in Mesopotamia *(Genesis 24)* and of the birth to them of twin sons, Jacob and Esau *(Genesis 25)*. The hero of the story is Jacob, although he does not actually appear a very heroic or noble figure since he cheated his brother out of his birthright *(Genesis 25:4–27:40)*. It is a notable fact about the Bible that it does not idealize its heroes, but shows them as real human beings.

Jacob was punished for his treachery by having to flee for his life. On the way, he came to Bethel where he rested his head upon a rock and, in a dream, saw angels ascending and descending upon a ladder which reached up into heaven *(Genesis 28)*. There God spoke to him and repeated the promises formerly made to Abraham, for Jacob was also to be the direct ancestor of all the people of Israel. In his flight, Jacob eventually came to Mesopotamia, where after many years of the hardest kind of labor, he married Leah and Rachel, who became the mothers of the twelve sons who, according to Hebrew tradition, were the ancestors of the twelve tribes of Israel *(Genesis 29, 30)*. At length he fled from the rule of his crafty and overbearing father-in-law, Laban, and took his family back with him to Palestine, where he was finally reconciled with his brother Esau *(Genesis 30-33)*. One of the strangest of all the stories in Genesis is one which tells how Jacob once wrestled with God all night and at last overcame Him and compelled God to give him His blessing *(Genesis 32:22-32)*. The story comes to us out of the mists of antiquity and we can only guess what its original meaning was, but at least in present form it purports to tell why Jacob's name was changed to Israel *(He who strives with God)*, the name by which his descendants would ever afterward be called.

## JOSEPH

ALL the rest of the Book of Genesis (chapters 37-50) is taken up by the story of Joseph, one of the twelve sons of Jacob, and his marvellous adventures in the land of Egypt. It is undoubtedly one of the great stories of world literature. The characters in it are real and human and, even today, we cannot help being moved by the pathos of the tale and carried along by its atmosphere of suspense and excitement. Joseph, the story tells us, had innocently aroused the jealousy of his brothers who, in the extremity of their hatred, sold him as a slave into the hands of Bedouin traders who were on their way to Egypt. There he was bought by Potiphar, the chief of Pharaoh's guard. Unfortunately, though innocent of any wrongdoing, Joseph awakened first the love and then the fear and hatred of Potiphar's wife, who succeeded in having him thrown into prison. Because God had given him the gift of interpreting dreams, he came at last to Pharaoh's attention and, interpreting the king's own dream, predicted the coming of a famine of unprecedented severity upon the land. Pharaoh, admiring his great gifts, appointed him as second in command over the kingdom, charged with the specific task of storing up an adequate supply of food for the long, lean years ahead. When at last the famine arrived, Joseph's brethren came down from Palestine in hope of securing food. There, after many adventures, both amusing and pathetic, they met and were reconciled to the brother they had treated so badly, but who dealt with them in such a gentle and forgiving way. *Ye meant evil against me,* he said, *but God meant it for good (Genesis 50:20).* At

length, Jacob and all his household were brought down
to Egypt and settled in the Delta, in *the land of Goshen*
*(Genesis 47:27)*. Finally, Jacob died, and after many
years, Joseph also *(Genesis 49:33; 50:26)*.

## HOW GOD BROUGHT ISRAEL OUT OF EGYPT

BETWEEN Genesis and EXODUS there is a gap of approximately four hundred years about which nothing is recorded *(Exodus 12:40)*. The gap is a significant one, since
it marks the transition from what we might call the world
of pre-history to the world of history. There are many
scholars who think that Abraham, Isaac, and Jacob are
simply personified tribes rather than real persons and that
their movements really represent the migrations of ancient
races or nations, but there can be no serious doubt, when
we come to Moses, that we are dealing with a man, one of
the great creative figures of all human history. It is with
Moses and the story of the Exodus that the history of the
people of Israel properly begins.

At the beginning of Exodus, the Israelites are laboring
as slaves for the Egyptians, as many other Asiatic tribes
did. They were cruelly oppressed and their lives were un-
speakably bitter *(Exodus 1)*. When an attempt was made
to stop the growth of the Hebrew population by killing
all the male children, the little boy Moses was providen-
tially saved by Pharaoh's daughter and raised as her own
son. When he grew to manhood, he killed an Egyptian
whom he found mistreating a Hebrew, and was forced to
flee for his life into the desert of Sinai. There he was received into the family of Jethro, the Midianite, and married his daughter *(Exodus 2)*. One day, while tending the

sheep of his father-in-law on the slopes of Mount Sinai (or Horeb, as it also is called) he received a wonderful revelation from God, who appeared to him in a mysterious burning bush and commanded him to return and lead the people of Israel out of Egypt. God revealed to Moses His name, Jehovah (or Yahweh, as many believe it was originally pronounced) and promised to support him in his efforts to win deliverance for his people *(Exodus 3, 4)*.

Moses, as God commanded him, returned to Egypt. There, after a series of unparalleled plagues, culminating in the death of all the first-born of Egypt, Pharaoh became convinced that a stronger God than the gods of Egypt was on the side of the Hebrews, and gave Moses permission to lead his people out into the desert. That evening, in accordance with God's command, they celebrated the sacred meal which was later to be an annual observance and which they called the Passover in commemoration of God's having passed over the houses of the Hebrews when the first-born of Egypt were slain *(Exodus 5-13)*. After they were on their way, Pharaoh regretted having let them go and pursued them with his armies but, attempting to follow them through the waters of the Red Sea, which had been wonderfully swept aside to make a passage for the children of Israel, he and all his host were drowned *(Exodus 14)*.

### ISRAEL AT SINAI

MOSES then led the people through the desert to Mount Sinai where they encamped, and he himself went up to the mountain top to receive the Law which would form the basis of God's Covenant with Israel *(Exodus 15-19)*. Beginning with chapter 20, most of the rest of the Book of

Exodus (with the exception of chapters 32, 33) consists of the various laws and regulations which, according to Hebrew tradition, were delivered to Moses at this time. The most important of these laws were, of course, the ten commandments *(Exodus 20:1-17;* also *Deuteronomy 5:1-21),* which stand at the head of them and constituted the basic moral law of Israel. Down to the present day, they remain the solid basis of all morality. Most of the laws in the rest of the Pentateuch are of comparatively minor importance and have to do with ceremonial and ritual matters rather than with morality. Many are, undoubtedly, much later than the time of Moses.

It always must be remembered that the story of these events was handed down orally for many generations before it was put in written form and in the course of time the dramatic nature of some of the events may have been exaggerated and certainly some things were interpreted in a sense different from the one which we should have given them. Thus, for instance, the slaying of the innocent children of the Egyptians seems to us a cruel act which we would hesitate to ascribe directly to God. It may be that the Hebrews of those remote times, who would not be troubled by such scruples, simply interpreted some pestilence which affected the Egyptian children as an act of God, done on their own behalf. The people of Israel still had a long way to go before they came to realize, with the prophet Ezekiel, that the good and righteous God does not desire the death even of the wicked. We meet with a similar problem, though not so acutely, in the story of the drowning of Pharaoh's army in the Red Sea. Recent scholarly studies tend to show that the story of the crossing of the Red Sea, in its original form, was simpler and less spectacular than the present story in Exodus would lead us to think, but this does not affect the essential historical truth of the narrative, which is that God, by delivering a band of feeble slaves out of the hands of their powerful oppressors, created for Himself a nation which was to be the special object of His love and care in the centuries ahead and from which the Redeemer of the world would one day come.

Exodus 32 and 33 tell how Moses, when he came down from the mountain after receiving the tables of the Law, found that the people had taken up the practice of idolatry while he was gone and were worshipping a golden calf which they had made. The story illustrates how hard it is for sinful man to remain true to God and how much easier it is for man to adore the things his own hand has made. Moses was so angered by what he saw that he broke the stone tablets which were in his hand. Later, the story recounts, they were replaced at God's command. The rest of Exodus describes the building of the tabernacle.

LEVITICUS contains mostly laws, of which the most important are those regulating the offering of sacrifice *(Leviticus 1-7)*, the ritual of the Day of Atonement *(Leviticus 16)*, and the fine humanitarian laws of chapter 19:11-18 from which our Lord drew the second great commandment, *Thou shalt love thy neighbor as thyself.*

## THE DESERT WANDERINGS

THE first part of the book of NUMBERS also consists mostly of laws, but the ancient epic of Israel's history is resumed at Numbers 10:11 which tells how the tribes left Sinai and moved up to the southern borders of Palestine, the land which God had promised them. They sent spies to look over the country, but were terrified at the report which was brought back of the military strength of the Canaanite inhabitants. They rebelled at Moses' leadership (thereby showing their lack of faith in God) and were condemned to spend forty years wandering in the desert *(Numbers 13, 14)*.

During this period they made their headquarters at Kadesh, an oasis south of Palestine, but eventually resumed their journey toward the Promised Land *(Numbers 20)*. They now turned eastward and went around the southern end of the Dead Sea into what today is called Transjordan and on the way met with numerous adventures as they encountered various nations long settled there. Most interesting of these is their experience with Balaam, a wizard whom the King of Moab had brought from far distant Mesopotamia to curse the Israelites. Balaam discovered, however, that God was on the side of the Hebrews, and every utterance which he intended to be a curse turned out to be a blessing *(Numbers 22, 23)*. The rest of Numbers consists largely of laws, with a little narrative material. Here is found the pathetic story of God's warning that Moses will not be permitted to lead the people into the Promised Land, and the command to appoint Joshua as his successor *(Numbers 27:12-22)*.

The Book of DEUTERONOMY is cast in the form of a farewell address by Moses to the people before they cross the Jordan River into Palestine. In it he summarizes the laws which God has given them. The laws of Deuteronomy are especially attractive to us because of the constant appeal they make to the motive of love toward God and man. The Ten Commandments stand at the head of the list *(Deuteronomy 5)*, and the following chapter *(Deuteronomy 6:4ff)* contains the great basic creed of Jewish religion (the so-called *Sheṁa,* Hear, O Israel, the Lord our God is one Lord) from which Jesus drew the first of the great commandments, *Thou shalt love the Lord thy God with all thy heart and with all thy soul and with all thy might.* Deuteronomy seems to have been one of our Lord's favorite Old Testament books. The Pentateuch comes to an end with the story of the death of Moses on a mountain top overlooking the Land of Promise, to the borders of which he had led his people *(Deuteronomy 34)*.

## HOW ISRAEL CONQUERED PALESTINE: JOSHUA

THE book of JOSHUA begins a series of historical books which deal with the fate of the people of Israel during the period from the death of Moses down to about the year 400 B.C., roughly about eight hundred years. The books from Joshua through II Kings have a certain unity of purpose and style and can be read in order just as they stand. The books I-II Chronicles, Ezra, and Nehemiah stand in some respects in a different category, as we shall see later (see page 70).

In the book of Joshua the ancient epic continues the story which began with the Exodus, and tells what befell Israel immediately after the death of Moses. Under the leadership of Joshua, the tribes crossed the Jordan River and there attacked the Canaanite city of Jericho. After seven days siege, the city fell in a strange and wonderful way, and, with the barbarism typical of the age, the entire population was slaughtered *(Joshua 1-6)*. The tribes next ventured an attack upon Ai, a city much nearer the center of Palestine, and, after an initial repulse, which they interpreted as a sign of God's displeasure with one of their number, they took this also *(Joshua 7, 8)*. Finally, in a series of battles, Joshua and the Israelites won decisive superiority over the Canaanites *(Joshua 9-11)* and the rest of the book describes the apportionment of the land amongst the tribes, and, finally, the death of Joshua (chapter 24).

### EARLY DAYS IN PALESTINE: THE JUDGES

THE book of JUDGES is made up of a series of fascinating old tales about life in the troubled times which followed immediately upon the conquest. The story told is not a consecutive one, but rather made up of a series of brief scenes, which give an invaluable picture of the life and manners of the times. Each story has its hero, a military leader (called a judge in the Hebrew sense of ruler) who arose in some great crisis of his people's life and delivered them from the hand of a foreign oppressor. The first one of importance was Ehud, who personally assassinated the king of Moab in the royal bedroom *(Judges 3:12-30)*. After him came Deborah, the only female judge, who inspired Barak to lead the Hebrews in a victorious uprising against the Canaanites which finally destroyed all semblance of Canaanite power *(Judges 4, 5)*. The Song of Deborah in chapter 5 is the oldest document of any length in the Hebrew language and one of the most stirring poems in any language.

The book goes on to tell of the courage of Gideon, who

46

drove a horde of Bedouin invaders from the land *(Judges 6, 7)*, and of Jephthah, a Robin Hood-like character, who belonged to the tribes east of the Jordan and freed his people from domination by the Ammonites *(Judges 10-12)*. The last and most famous of the judges was Samson, a strong man of somewhat childish mentality, who was champion of the people of Israel against the rising power of the Philistines. The story of his tragic involvement with an unscrupulous woman, Delilah, who betrayed him to his enemies, and of his heroic death, is one of the great stories of all literature *(Judges 13-16)*. The heroes of the book of Judges are not religious leaders and are sometimes admirable only in the sense in which all courageous men are admirable, but through the whole of the book there runs the theme which is so basic to Old Testament thought, that a nation is really weak only when it is disloyal to God. When the children of Israel were on God's side, He was on theirs; when they forsook Him, He forsook them.

The little book of RUTH is a beautiful, romantic novelette, set in the time of the judges though written eight or nine centuries later. It is really a tract against race prejudice. Its heroine, after whom the book is named, is a generous-spirited Moabite woman who proves herself to be as fine a person and as devoted a worshipper of the true God as any Hebrew. The concluding verses make the point that this noble foreign woman was the ancestress of King David.

# Historical Books: *II. The Hebrew Kingdoms*

ALTHOUGH the next two books of the Bible bear the name of Samuel, in whose days and by whose authority the Hebrew monarchy was established, their real hero is David. The situation at the beginning of I SAMUEL is the same as that in the time of Samson. The Hebrew tribes, who had been settled in the hill country of the land of Canaan for about two hundred years and had won dominion over it but had never been unified under a single ruler or government, were threatened by the Philistines, a nation which had settled about the same time on the coastal plain in the west of Palestine. The Philistines gradually pressed up into the hills and, as they did so, aroused the sleeping energies of Israel to resist them. It was the kind of situation which called for unified leadership and thereby actually created the monarchy.

## HOW ISRAEL BECAME A KINGDOM: SAMUEL AND SAUL

THE first part of the story is dominated by the figure of Samuel, who, from one standpoint, was the last of the Judges, but, in contrast to his predecessors, was a priest and a religious, rather than a military leader. The familiar story of his birth and childhood upbringing in the temple at Shiloh is told in chapters 1-3, while chapters 4-7 describe two incidents in the Philistine wars after he had arrived at manhood and assumed the leadership of the people. The precarious general situation led inevitably to the demand for a king who could be a center of unity for the nation and lead it in battle. There were certain obvious objections to introducing the institution of monarchy among a people who were by tradition and culture as democratic as the Hebrews, but Samuel at last consented to the demand and believed that he had God's permission to do so *(I Samuel 8)*.

Chapter 9 introduces the man who was destined to be the first king of Israel, Saul, a noble though tragic figure. We first see him as a young man in search of his father's lost asses. When he went to consult Samuel as to their whereabouts, he learned with amazement that God had destined him to be king and he was later anointed to that high office *(I Samuel 9, 10)*. We then see him as Israel's leader in war, first against the Ammonites in a battle in which he proved his mettle *(I Samuel 11)*, and later against the Philistines, when his son Jonathan showed himself a worthy child of his father *(I Samuel 13, 14)*.

Unfortunately, however, the temperaments of Saul and Samuel did not agree, and Samuel felt that Saul had

**49**

shown himself proud and undependable on more than one occasion *(I Samuel 13:8-15; 15)*. Because Saul, by disobeying simple and direct commands *(I Samuel 15:22, 23)* had proved himself unworthy to command others, Samuel declared the kingdom must be taken from him and conferred on another. Among the children of Jesse, a citizen of Bethlehem, Samuel found the young boy, David, whom he instantly recognized as the divinely chosen successor of Saul. David was shortly after this introduced to the court of Saul because of his gifts as a musician. His songs had power to soothe the wild rages to which the darkening mind of Saul was now becoming subject *(I Samuel 16)*. David is also presented to us as a fearless warrior in the famous story of the slaying of the Philistine giant, Goliath *(I Samuel 17)*, an event which led to his marriage to the daughter of King Saul *(I Samuel 18)*. The following chapters tell of the rapidly developing jealousy between the King and his now famous and popular son-in-law and the fine friendship which grew up between David and Jonathan.

Saul's insane jealousy finally led David to flee for his life *(I Samuel 19-21)*. For a considerable time he led the life of an outlaw as the head of a band of malcontents in the wild region around Adullam in southern Palestine, but even during this period showed the essential nobility of his character by twice sparing the life of Saul, when tricks of fate delivered the King into his hands *(I Samuel 22-26)*. At last David tired of this life and settled down in comparative comfort and security under the protection of Saul's Philistine enemies *(I Samuel 27)*. The first book of Samuel closes with the death of Saul and three of his sons in a great battle with the Philistines. Perhaps the most pathetic thing in the book is the picture of Saul, a man broken in mind and spirit, seeking guidance from the witch of En-dor, and receiving only assurance of disaster *(I Samuel 28-31).*

## DAVID BECOMES KING

II SAMUEL opens with the scene in which David hears the news of the death of the King and his sons, and the first chapter contains the poignant lament of David over Saul which is one of the most precious fragments of ancient Hebrew literature. Here, more than anywhere else, we feel ourselves in touch with the mind and warm humanity of David. On Saul's death, David assumed the crown of Southern Israel, although one of Saul's weaker surviving sons remained upon the throne in the north and east. When this poor-spirited creature was finally assassinated by members of his own household, David almost automatically became king over all Israel *(II Samuel 2:1-5; 4).*

David was undoubtedly a political genius, as Saul had never been, and immediately set to work to consolidate and to organize his kingdom. Although little of the detail is told, it is clear that he finally put an end to the Philistine menace *(II Samuel 5:17-25)* and gave Israel a sense of security in its own land. His most significant single act, however, one of immeasurable consequence to all later generations, was the selection of a new capital, Jerusalem. Both because it was centrally located and because it had never been a Hebrew city before and therefore occupied a neutral position with reference to the various tribes, each jealous of its own territory and traditions, it was peculiarly suited to provide a center of unity for the young nation. Until this time, it had been held by a Canaanite clan called the Jebusites, but David captured it with a clever stratagem. He not only made it the center of his political administration, but also, by bringing the ark there, made it a center of religious devotion *(II Samuel 5, 6)*. David wished also to build a great temple there, but the prophet Nathan discouraged him from doing so on the ground that the God of Israel had no need of such a dwelling *(II Samuel 7)*. David, however, had laid the foundations of a great structure of faith and devotion which was to grow up around Jerusalem, for it was destined to become not simply the capital of a kingdom, but a spiritual idea, the visible symbol of man's longing for the eternal city of God. David was successful in almost everything he touched and the little kingdom which he had inherited soon became a great and wealthy empire, holding sovereignty over most of the surrounding peoples *(II Samuel 8)*. It was this great success of David, evidence of God's special favor, along with his unquestioned personal attractiveness, that made him to all later generations the ideal king and the image as well as the ancestor of the future Messiah.

### DAVID'S WEAKNESSES

On the other hand, the character of David was by no means unblemished, and with an honesty typical of the Bible, the Old Testament presents the dark side of his nature along with the bright. Most of the remaining chapters of II Samuel are concerned with David's private weaknesses and failures, which stood out in such marked contrast to his public success. We learn first of his treachery toward his faithful servant, Uriah the Hittite, whose death he accomplished because of his own love for Bathsheba, Uriah's beautiful wife. We also learn of his penitence when Nathan the prophet accused him of the crime to his face *(II Samuel 11, 12).*

David's greatest weakness lay in the foolish indulgence with which he treated his own children. His failure as a father appears most acutely in the lengthy and sordid story of Absalom's revolt. Absalom was one of his favorite sons, a young man who had inherited all his father's political acuteness and personal charm, but none of his basic moral seriousness. He accepted all that David was willing to do for him, but returned nothing of his affection. At last he conceived the plan of stirring up dissension among his father's subjects so as to win the crown for himself. When the time was ripe he raised a revolt in the south, and, when he began the march upon Jerusalem, was so well established in the favor of the people that David was forced to flee to Transjordan. David was fortunate in having a wise general and clever councillors and, though Absalom won the first move, he lost the decisive battle. In the end, he was ignominiously murdered by Joab, his father's acute, but ruthless, commander. Even in the moment of victory, however, David's self-centered lamentations over the death of his contemptible son almost lost him the favor of his loyal supporters, and it was necessary for Joab to recall him to his senses *(II Samuel 13-19).*

## SOLOMON: THE MAGNIFICENT MONARCH

THE two books of the Kings deal with the period from the death of David to the end of the monarchy. I KINGS begins with an account of the palace intrigues which began while David was still living, but sick and senile. Bathsheba, by a clever stroke, succeeded in having her son, Solomon, recognized by David as his successor before his older brother Adonijah could fully organize the forces which were favorable to him (*I Kings 1:5–2:12*).

On his accession to the throne, Solomon quickly seized the opportunity to rid himself of possible adversaries (*I Kings 2:13-46*). In this he was merely following the same cynical policy which has prevailed in oriental courts down to the present day. Solomon had the good fortune to succeed to a kingdom which was at the height of its power. Although he seems to have had little of the kind of ability which made his father so successful in war and in political administration, yet he obtained a great reputation in his own time and in later generations for wisdom, and several stories are told to illustrate his gifts as a ruler (*I Kings 3 and 10*). The prosperity of his reign was largely due to three factors:

The excellence of his inherited political organization

The absence at this time of any great world power able to challenge the position of Israel

His own apparently real gifts for trade and commerce.

Unlike his father, he was primarily a man of business, who exploited the resources at his command in order to increase the wealth and external splendor of his kingdom. He was actually the first king of Israel who attempted to imitate the luxuriousness of other oriental monarchies. Saul had lived as a simple countryman, and even David was so much concerned with strengthening and enlarging the kingdom that he had little time left in which to put on the airs of a king. But Solomon lived in splendid state and embarked upon a great program of public building, chiefly designed to enhance his own magnificence. His two greatest buildings were, of course, the royal palace and the temple. In subsequent history, the latter was destined to have the greatest importance, but there is little doubt that in Solomon's mind the building of the temple was merely incidental to the creation of a whole complex of royal buildings *(I Kings 5-9)*. In this he was departing very far from the simplicity of ancient Hebrew life and the traditional religious and social ideals of his people. These great works could be completed only at the cost of heavy taxation and by the use of slave labor, and the ultimate result of his policy was the weakening and ultimate dissolution of the strong, unified kingdom which he had inherited. With all his superficial cleverness, which is what his contemporaries meant by his wisdom, he is actually a model of what a king, or any man, ought not to be, for his chief concern was not personal character, but material wealth; not the things which are eternal, but the things which are temporal. Tradition was more merciful to him than history and in later times he was commonly regarded as a royal philosopher and the author of several profound books on the nature of reality and the good life, Proverbs, Ecclesiastes, The Wisdom of Solomon, etc., as well as a poet, the author of The Song of Solomon, The Psalms of Solomon, etc.

**DIVISION OF THE KINGDOM: THE KINGDOM OF ISRAEL**

THE unhappy results of Solomon's short-sighted policy were already evident in a series of revolts which broke out even during his own lifetime *(I Kings 11:14-42)*. Immediately after his death, when his son Rehoboam attempted to continue in his footsteps, the kingdom was torn asunder by violent rebellion and by far the greater part of it became an independent monarchy under a new king, Jeroboam *(I Kings 12)*. From this time onward, there were two Hebrew kingdoms: Israel in the north of Palestine, the later capital of which was Samaria; and Judah, now a small and comparatively insignificant kingdom in the south, which, nevertheless, still possessed the great advantage of having Jerusalem for its capital and the family of David for its rulers. In the period which immediately follows, it is the northern kingdom, Israel, which is the center of interest, because of its size and importance and because its internal history was far more marked by violence and conflict than that of the little kingdom of Judah which continued to move rather quietly within its own small orbit.

### ELIJAH

A LITTLE less than a hundred years after the division of the kingdoms, a great conflict, partly religious and partly political and social, broke out in the northern kingdom. The king who occupied the throne was Ahab, a strong and, in his own way, very able ruler. The trouble, however, seems largely to have arisen over the activities of his Phoenician wife, Jezebel, who desired to introduce the religion and social institutions of her own nation among the people of Israel. Ahab was apparently clay in Jezebel's strong and resolute hands *(I Kings 16:29-34)*. Fortunately, in the providence of God, she was not allowed to have her own way and a champion of Israel's ancient religion and

56

morality arose to oppose her. This was Elijah the Tish-
bite, a prophet, a stern and uncompromising fighter for
what he believed to be right. Many tales were told of his
courage and of the way in which God supported his endeavors *(I Kings 17-21)*. The most dramatic of these is
that which tells of his contest with the prophets of Jezebel's Phoenician god called Baal at a great outdoor gath-
ering on the summit of Mount Carmel. The 450 prophets
of Baal, goaded to frenzy by the rough humor of Elijah's
taunts, were unable to evoke any response from their god,
but, when at last they gave up the attempt, Elijah had no
difficulty in getting an answer from Jehovah, the God of
Israel, and in bringing to an end the drought which had
long afflicted the land *(I Kings 18)*. Although he was successful in the conflict, he aroused the implacable hatred of
Jezebel and was forced to flee in order to save his life.
Going off into the desert to Horeb, the mountain where
Jehovah in former times had revealed Himself to Moses,
Elijah received a commission to continue his battle and
overthrow the dynasty of Ahab. He was also to insure the
continuance of his efforts by selecting someone to carry
on the work. On his way back from Horeb he came to
Elisha as the latter was plowing a field and chose him on
the spot to be his disciple and successor *(I Kings 19)*. His
next great conflict with Ahab and Jezebel arose over a
matter of social justice. Jezebel had instigated her husband
to act tyrannically in a way which was in accord with the
customs of the rest of the ancient orient, where kings had
absolute power, but was contrary to the democratic spirit
of Israel, where kings had only limited powers and even
the humblest citizen had certain inalienable rights. By

fraudulent accusation and judicial murder, Ahab took possession of the vineyard of his neighbor, Naboth the Jezreelite, but when he went to inspect his property, Elijah met him face to face and pronounced God's curse upon him and his entire family *(I Kings 21)*.

## ELISHA

FINALLY it came Elijah's turn to die and II KINGS 2 tells the story of his ascent to heaven in a whirlwind, with chariot and horses of fire. Elisha immediately took over the work which his master had left unfinished. As was the case with Elijah, many wonderful stories were told about him and the miracles which he performed. Most of his miracles were acts of kindness to people who were sick or in trouble *(II Kings 3-8)*. One of the most famous of the stories about Elisha is that of the healing of the leper, Naaman, an official in the court of the King of Syria, who had to learn the lesson of strict obedience to God's will even in things which seem unimportant and even humiliating *(II Kings 5)*. Elisha believed that God's help never fails His faithful worshippers. Another famous story tells how, once, when trapped in a besieged city, he caused the eyes of his faint-hearted servant to be opened in order to see the hills round about full of the horses and chariots of the Lord *(II Kings 6:8-19)*. The climax of Elisha's career came when he at last instigated a successful revolt against the dynasty of Ahab and placed a new king, Jehu, upon the throne. Joram, Ahab's son and successor, was assassinated along with his friend the King of Judah and the Queen mother Jezebel *(II Kings 9, 10)*. It is a dreadful story and there can be no doubt that Jehu, the actual agent of the revolt, who became the new king, was acting rather for reasons of personal ambition than for the honor of the God of Israel.

We cannot but feel that Elisha chose the wrong means in order to attain his undoubtedly good end. We can justify it only by saying that the conscience of the times was not yet sufficiently sensitive to understand that loyalty to God can never justify treachery and violence. We should also remember that Hebrew history itself passed an unfavorable judgment upon Jehu, and that Hosea, a prophet who lived only a century later, denounced the bloody deed of Jehu and declared that his dynasty, too, was doomed *(Hosea 1:4)*. We can see that the years which followed Elisha, although rather obscure from the point of view of actual history, must have been a time when a new spirit was stirring in the mind and conscience of Israel. This was soon to find expression in the work of the great writing prophets.

## THE END OF THE NORTHERN KINGDOM

THE remaining history of the northern kingdom can be told rather briefly. It had one long period of prosperity under the rule of a descendant of Jehu, Jeroboam II, in the closing years of whose reign the first two literary prophets, Amos and Hosea, began their work *(II Kings 14:23-29)*. For the moment it is enough to say that both predicted the imminent end of the Kingdom of Israel. Amos did so on the ground that the nation had forsaken the principles of social justice; Hosea, on the ground that it had failed in loyalty to God. The great influence which the literary prophets were to have from this time on was

59

no doubt due to the fact that these first prophecies of doom came true. For the first time Israel found herself threatened by a great world empire, Assyria. She rushed around frantically trying to save her independence, even going so far as to declare war on little Judah to try and force her into an anti-Assyrian alliance. Her fate, however, was sealed. After the death of Jeroboam II, the kingdom was torn apart by intrigue and rebellion *(II Kings 15:8-37)* and so weakened that at length her capital, Samaria, fell to the Assyrian armies (721 B.C.) and the Kingdom of Israel came to an end forever. Many of her people were taken into exile and are known to history as the ten lost tribes of Israel *(II Kings 17:1-6)*. Actually they were not lost in the usual sense of the term, but were gradually assimilated among the people of the lands where they settled. The people who were left in the old territory of Israel, mostly of the lower classes, became partially mixed with certain pagan peoples, and were the ancestors of the Samaritans whom we meet in the New Testament *(II Kings 17:24-41)*.

# Historical Books: *III. Exile and Return*

LIFE in Judah had been going on all during this period, but much more quietly. There were no attempts to overthrow the ruling family. Some of the kings such as Asa *(I Kings 15:9-24)* and Jehoshaphat *(I Kings 22:41-50)* were worthy successors of David, while others, particularly the infamous Athaliah, the daughter of Ahab and Jezebel, would have been a disgrace to any kingdom *(II Kings 11)*. Much of the time Judah, because of her small size and dependent condition, was either allied to Israel or actually tributary to her. Because she was in a more remote geographical situation than Israel, Judah was not so early drawn into the stream of world history as was her neighbor to the north. She lived in a quiet backwater and was probably a century or so behind Israel in the general level of her cultural life. It illustrates a principle which frequently holds true in God's dealings with men that comparatively obscure and backward Judah was finally given the task of furthering the divine purpose among men rather than wealthy and powerful Israel.

## AHAZ THE KING, AND ISAIAH THE PROPHET

As Israel was tottering toward disaster, she sought support in a policy of strong alliances with neighboring States. Judah, because of her natural weakness and a strong strain of isolationism in her national character, refused to join in any union of States directed against the Assyrians, and as a result was attacked by the armies of Israel and its nearest northern neighbor, Syria. This is known to Biblical history as the Syro-Ephraimite War (Ephraim means Israel).

Ahaz, a king whose thinking ran almost entirely along political rather than religious lines, was alarmed at the situation and, anxiously casting around for help, sent messengers to Assyria begging for armed intervention *(II Kings 16)*. As so frequently happened in Old Testament history, the emergency produced a great spiritual leader who was able to interpret the meaning of the crisis and give counsel as to the appropriate way to meet it. The man was ISAIAH and the part he played in the situation is described in the seventh chapter of his book. His message was one of simple trust in God and avoidance of all merely political and military maneuvers: *If ye will not believe, ye shall not be established (Isaiah 7:9)*. Ahaz did not follow Isaiah's advice and won the day in his own fashion by getting the help of the Assyrians, but only at the cost of paying heavy tribute and making himself a vassal of the Assyrian king, thus saving himself from one situation by precipitating himself into a worse.

62

Isaiah's ministry as a prophet, unlike that of the northern prophets, Amos and Hosea, extended over a very long time. It had begun in the very year in which Ahaz came to the throne *(Isaiah 6)* and was destined to continue through the entire reign of his son and successor, Hezekiah, a period of at least forty years *(II Kings 18-20)*. He was on good terms with Hezekiah, who was a reforming monarch and was accounted by later historians one of the best kings of Judah. Hezekiah, however, did not in all particulars follow Isaiah's counsel and, on one significant occasion, took a precisely opposite line. In spite of having lived through the declining years of the Kingdom of Israel, and having seen the fate of Samaria, Hezekiah rebelled against his Assyrian overlord, Sennacherib, and at length found himself besieged in Jerusalem, the rest of the country occupied by enemy troops and all hope apparently gone. At this crisis, as at the earlier one in his father's reign, Isaiah came forth with his message of faith in God and assured the king that the Assyrians would never take the city.[1] And the Assyrians never did! Exactly what happened is not entirely certain, but both the Bible and secular history testify that Jerusalem was not taken. The armies of Sennacherib, when the city seemed already within their grasp, suddenly picked up their tents and returned in haste to Assyria *(II Kings 19:35-37)*. Thus Isaiah's

---

[1] It is sometimes inferred that Isaiah taught "the doctrine of the inviolability of Zion," *viz.* that because Jerusalem was God's City, He would never allow it to be captured, regardless of the moral condition of the inhabitants. It is difficult to believe that Isaiah intended his teaching to be interpreted in so mechanical a way. His doctrine of faith and his conviction as to the manner in which God would act in the particular crises of 735 and 701 B.C. should not be distorted into a rigid and essentially immoral dogma.

teaching was vindicated. He seems, however, to have died shortly afterward and Jewish tradition says that he was martyred, "sawn asunder," in the reign of Hezekiah's successor, Manasseh. Judah also had another prophet, who lived in the time of Isaiah, the peasant prophet, MICAH, who preached in the southern kingdom the same message of God's demand for social justice which Amos preached in Israel.

### THE EVIL REIGN OF MANASSEH

MANASSEH, the son of Hezekiah, is regarded by the Jewish historians as the worst of the kings of Judah, and with good reason, since he completely reversed the wise policies of his father and voluntarily entered into a new alliance with Assyria, a course which involved cultural and religious, as well as political, ties. He persecuted those who insisted upon undeviating loyalty to Jehovah, the God of Israel, and either killed the prophets or forced them to work as a kind of underground movement. This general state of things continued under Manasseh and his successors for more than fifty years. Consequently there is no prophetic literature from this period and one can see how easily, just from the human point of view, the treasure which had been committed to Israel, the revelation of the just and holy God, might have been lost beyond recovery *(II Kings 21:1-18)*. The Spirit of God, however, was at work through His chosen servants and when at last, Josiah, regarded by the historians as the best of all the kings of Judah, came to the throne, the situation was dramatically reversed, the prophets were encouraged to renew their activity and every effort was made to restore the religion of

Israel in all its purity. Assyria at this time had suffered a series of blows and was on the verge of passing forever from the scene of world history, so Josiah had no hesitation in throwing off his allegiance to her and declaring the complete political and religious independence of his nation.

## JOSIAH'S GREAT REFORM

ALL this at last came to a head in Josiah's eighteenth year, 621 B.C., when some workman, engaged in restoring the Temple which Manasseh had allowed to fall into disrepair, discovered a book of the laws of God which had apparently been long lost *(II Kings 22)*. This is now generally believed to have been the Book of Deuteronomy.[2] Josiah thereupon began a great reform movement with the purpose of securing the strict observance of these laws.

The most important provision in this particular law code was that sacrifice must not be offered to God anywhere except in Jerusalem *(Deuteronomy 12:1-7)* so Josiah ordered the destruction of all other shrines and altars in the land *(II Kings 23)*. When worship was being carried on at so many little local sanctuaries, it had never been possible entirely to eliminate the unsavoury practices of the old Canaanite fertility cult, with its repulsive emphasis upon sexuality, from the religious life of the people of Israel, but now there would no longer be any danger of contamination from this source since all worship was to

---

[2] Most scholars believe that this book, a compilation of mostly ancient laws, but revised in a new spirit, actually had been drawn up secretly as the program of the reforming party in the reign of Manasseh and perhaps intentionally put where the workmen would find it so that it might be brought dramatically and forcefully to the attention of the king.

be under the direct control and supervision of the re-forming priesthood in Jerusalem. This decree of Josiah did more than any other single thing to make Jerusalem the holy city of the Hebrews.

Josiah's reformation was epoch-making in many ways, but nothing in it was perhaps more important than the fact that a book was now declared to be the sole source of authority in faith and morals and was accepted as such by the entire nation. This was the real beginning of the Bible, and it is, in one sense, quite correct to say that the Book of Deuteronomy is the first book in the Bible, the first, that is, to be accepted authoritatively as the Word of God.

### THE PROPHET JEREMIAH AND JUDAH'S LAST DAYS

WHEN Josiah lifted the ban on the prophets, new prophetic books began to appear. The first was that of ZEPHANIAH, who wrote about some threat to world peace, which many scholars identify with the invasion of barbarian hordes, the Scythians, who were terrifying the whole Near East in the early years of Josiah's reign. The greatest prophet of the age and, some would say, of any age was Jeremiah, a young country boy, who felt that God had called him to go up to Jerusalem to be a religious leader to His people *(Jeremiah 1)*. His prophetic ministry, like that of Isaiah, was a long one, and lasted through all the years yet remaining to the Kingdom of Judah. His message was a consistent one: *Doom is coming upon the kingdom of Judah! (e.g. Jeremiah 4:5-9; 37:10)*. There were, of course, many facets to his message and his contribution to the re-ligious life of humanity is immeasurable, but, for his own

66

time, the essence of his proclamation was simply this: God is about to bring judgment upon His people for their age-long failure to be loyal to Him and to deal justly with each other *(Jeremiah 2:29-37)*.

In the years which followed the beginning of Jeremiah's prophetic ministry, his message grew stale to his hearers through much repetition and there seemed little in the objective situation of Judah to justify his sombre tones. Indeed it looked as though Judah was on the verge of a golden age. The Empire of Assyria had collapsed and King Josiah evidently thought the time was ripe to re-establish the kingdom of David in all its ancient extent. Jeremiah, however, was not judging the future by the superficial evidence of external conditions. He was deeply in touch with the moral life of his people and he could feel within it that corruption of the national morale which meant that disaster and death were imminent *(Jeremiah 13:23-27)*.

Toward the end of the seventh century, the form in which the doom would come began to be more and more evident. The history of the period is very complex, but it is enough to say that the good king Josiah was killed in battle and succeeded by his son, Jehoiakim, a thoroughly self-centered politician and the willing tool of any foreign power strong enough to claim his allegiance *(Jeremiah 22:13-19)*. Shortly after this, Babylon succeeded in establishing her claim to be Assyria's successor as ruler of the oriental world, and Jehoiakim quite voluntarily submitted to her overlordship. Eventually, however, having misjudged his resources and misled by promises of help from the Egyptians, he rebelled and attempted to set himself up as an independent monarch. Nebuchadnezzar, the Babylonian king, immediately marched against him, captured the city, 597 B.C., and carried away the most influential among the people to captivity in Babylon. Jehoiakim died before the city fell, and his son Jehoiachin came to the throne just in time to be carried away by the Babylonians. His uncle, Zedekiah, a well-meaning but indecisive individual, succeeded him as king, and, ten years later, allowed the same bad advice and the same false promises of foreign assistance to precipitate him foolishly into another rebellion against the Babylonians. This time, the Babylonians had completely lost patience and when Jerusalem was captured after a long siege, 586 B.C., the horrors of which are described in the Book of LAMENTATIONS (e.g., chapter 4), Nebuchadnezzar ordered it razed to the foundations, including the walls and the temple of Solomon, so as to make further revolt forever impossible. This time a much larger part of the population, though by no means the whole of it, was carried into exile. Thus Jeremiah's dark prophecies came true and the Hebrew kingdom was at an end. The Babylonian Exile had begun. This is the story told in II Kings 23:26–25:21.

Two more of the prophetic books belong in this period. The Book of HABAKKUK is an attempt to wrestle with the moral problem created by the rapid succession of victories achieved by the ungodly Babylonians, Chaldeans. The Book of EZEKIEL is the work of a prophet who in 597 B.C. went to Babylonia among the first captives and there followed, and commented upon, the progress of events in Palestine. He also continued to prophesy for a number of years after the Exile began.

68

THIS might very well have been the end of Israel and of the religious truths which had been committed to her keeping. But God still had a great work, the greatest, for her to do. His Spirit was at work among the exiles in Babylonia, stirring up in them a great consciousness of their own past glories and a sense of greater things yet to come. During the Exile, the Jews ceased to be a nation in the former sense of the word and began to become what God intended them to be: a spiritual community, a Church. When the religion of sacrifice and Temple was gone, the religion of the Book and the synagogue was born, a religion which could be practiced anywhere in the world, not merely on the soil of Palestine. Thus in the Exile there began to take place that great expansion of the horizons of Judaism which was a necessary pre-condition for the rise within it of the Christian Church.

## AFTER THE BABYLONIAN EXILE: THE SECOND ISAIAH

EVENTUALLY the Exile came to an end. The Babylonian Empire fell before the rising power of Persia, and when Cyrus, the Persian king, entered Babylon, 539 B.C., one of his first acts was a decree permitting the Jews who were settled in Babylonia to return to their homeland. The progress of Cyrus had been anxiously followed by the exiled Jews and one of their number, an anonymous prophet, wrote some of the most beautiful chapters in the Old Testament at this time, telling of the glorious things God was about to do for his people. These prophecies are now attached to the end of the Book of Isaiah and lacking a better name, the author is commonly called the Second Isaiah.

# HOW THE TEMPLE WAS REBUILT

WE have only fragmentary information about the period which follows and have to depend largely on the rather confused and episodic story told in the Books of Ezra and Nehemiah. These two books are merely the concluding part of a great historical work which begins with I and II CHRONICLES. The author of this four-volume outline of world history wrote many centuries after the events and had very little material with which to work. For the early part of his story *(I-II Chronicles)*, he merely rewrote the Books of Samuel and Kings in accordance with his own somewhat peculiar philosophy of history, idealizing the characters, sometimes elaborating, sometimes condensing, the narrative. These first two books have little new to tell us, but the last two, Ezra and Nehemiah, with all their deficiencies as history, are invaluable for the unique, though fitful, light they throw on the obscure centuries which followed the Exile.

EZRA 1-4 describes the return of the exiles under the royal prince Zerubbabel and their first attempts to reëstablish the worship of God in Jerusalem. Some eighteen years after the return, the prophets HAGGAI and ZECHARIAH stirred up the energies of the people to begin the rebuilding of the Temple and in 516 B.C. it was completed *(Ezra 5, 6)*. Ezra himself, according to the book which bears his name, *(Ezra 7-10)*, was a scribe (the first to receive the name) who came to Jerusalem from Babylon about the middle of the following century and carried on a campaign to reawaken the religious zeal of the Jews, especially by putting an end to marriages with foreign women, which, he felt, were destroying the unity of the people of Israel and the integrity of their religion.

He also brought with him a Book of the Law *(Nehemiah 8-10)* which most scholars identify, at least in part, with the document in the Pentateuch called P. It was evidently in the main a book of detailed instructions with regard to life and worship and was immediately accepted by the people as of binding authority. It was not long before this book was combined with the older documents J and E and the Book of Deuteronomy to form the Pentateuch, the first five books of the Bible as it is today. These five books together with the various commentaries which grew up about them are what the New Testament calls "the law" for, from the time of Ezra on, they constituted the fundamental law of the Jewish religion. Because they had to be interpreted, there grew up a special class of students of the Law, who became the real religious leaders of the Jews and were called scribes or rabbis. This kind of religion, which centered in the Law and the work of the rabbis, is what is called Judaism and was the religion in which Jesus and St. Paul were nurtured. Thus the work begun by Ezra was of almost inestimable importance.

The other great man of this age was NEHEMIAH, a layman who had risen to a high position in the Persian court and chose to exercise his great influence for the good of his people. He became governor of the Jews in 444 B.C. and immediately set to work to restore the city walls of Jerusalem. In doing so he aroused the enmity of the people who lived in the north, around Samaria and Shechem, and the final breach between the Jews and Samaritans is to be dated from about this time. He also attempted to purify and consolidate the religious life of the people by seeing that the religious taxes were paid, the Sabbath properly observed, and marriages with foreign women forbidden. How necessary Nehemiah's reform was, we see from the Book of MALACHI, which dates from the period immediately before his coming to Jerusalem. Despite a certain narrowness in his vision, Nehemiah emerges as a really good type of the devout and consecrated layman. Many scholars believe that the chronology of these books is incorrect and that the work of Ezra is actually to be dated about fifty years after Nehemiah.

To us, the almost fanatical devotion of Ezra and Nehemiah to the Jewish nation and their violent opposition to any compromise with the surrounding Gentile world seems a severe limitation on their greatness and an unfortunate narrowing down of the broad vision which is evident in some of the earlier prophets. We should recognize, though, that the Jewish religion, the religion of a small and impoverished community, could hardly have survived through the difficult years which were to follow, if it had not been for the uncompromising loyalty to the nation and the traditional religion engendered by such men as these and their equally "narrow-minded" followers. They undoubtedly played a real and very important role for the time in which they lived, and we should regret only that the exclusiveness which was a necessity for a particular age still remained when the crisis was past. Even in the times following Ezra and Nehemiah, however, there were protests against the extreme views to which their teaching gave rise. Thus in the Book of JONAH, we have an amusing caricature of a narrow-minded prophet who cannot conceive that God is interested in anyone except Jews, and in the Book of Ruth (see page 47) the attractive portrait of a woman who, although of non-Jewish origin, proved herself capable of sacrificial devotion and genuine religious feeling. These two books show that the more liberal strain in Jewish religion was by no means dead. It was, of course, to this strain that Christianity attached itself.

## AFTER THE HISTORICAL BOOKS

Very little is known of the centuries 400-200 B.C., although most of the books of the Bible, apart from the Pentateuch, actually came into being or were edited in their final form during this period. From other sources than the Bible, we know that Palestine, like the rest of the oriental world, passed under a series of new rulers when at last the Persian Empire was overthrown by Alexander the Great. From about 333 B.C. Palestine was a part of the Greek world and the influence of Greek language, thought, and culture upon the Jewish people was enormous. The fact that the New Testament was written in Greek is one of the most striking evidences of this. Greek culture became so popular that for a time it looked as though the traditional culture and religion of Israel would be entirely lost. Out of this situation grew the last great crisis of Israel before the Christian era.

## THE HEROIC STRUGGLE OF THE MACCABEES

If the infiltration of Greek culture had continued to be a gradual thing, it might have succeeded in obliterating the old national culture of Israel, but things were suddenly

73

brought to a dramatic head when a Grecian king, Antiochus Epiphanes, who ruled over the Seleucid (Syrian) Empire, one of the kingdoms into which Alexander's world-empire had broken up after his death, attempted forcibly to suppress the religion of the Jews. The story of the thrilling battle for national survival which followed is told in the books of the Apocrypha called I and II MACCABEES. Antiochus had forbidden the practice of Judaism and had actually set up a pagan altar, "the abomination of desolation," in the temple at Jerusalem, not realizing with what kind of people he had to deal. The devout nucleus of the nation rose against him in violent revolt under the leadership of Judas Maccabeus and gradually drove the Syrian forces out of the land. It was in this period that the Book of DANIEL was written, in order to encourage the Jews to fight bravely against their foreign oppressors by showing them, on the one hand *(Daniel 1-6)* how courageously their ancestors in the days of the Babylonian Exile had stood up for their faith, and on the other hand, *(Daniel 7-14)* how certain they could be of victory since God was on their side and had already determined the outcome *(Daniel 7:27).*

## THE HASMONEAN KINGDOM

THE Jews were entirely victorious under the leadership of Judas and other members of his family; the temple was restored to the worship of Jehovah, 165 B.C., and a few years later a Jewish kingdom was once more established in Palestine with the family of the Maccabees, now called the Hasmoneans, as the ruling dynasty. This began a period of aggressive nationalism such as had not been possible for more than three hundred years and would not be paralleled again until the rise of modern Zionism. It reached its highest pitch in the forcible conversion to Judaism of some of the Jews' near neighbors to the north and south, especially the Idumeans. In all probability, the Book of ESTHER was written in this age, as no book in the Old Testament is so completely a product of unrestrained, purely secular, nationalism as this. It is a romantic novelette laid in the days of the Persian Empire, which reaches its climax with the slaughter by the Jews of seventy-five thousand Gentiles! The chief values of this book are literary and historical. It is an exciting story, well told, and gives an insight into the mind of many of the Jewish people at this remarkable period in their history. The Apocryphal Book of JUDITH is of much the same character and was probably written about the same time.

### THE ROMAN EMPIRE: HEROD THE GREAT

THE independent Hasmonean kingdom, however, did not have long to live. In 64 B.C. Syria and Palestine became a part of the Roman Empire. Eventually Herod the Great, an Idumean whose people had been converted to Judaism at the sword's point a short time before his birth, succeeded by an almost incredibly cynical combination of perfidy, brutality, and political shrewdness in getting himself recognized as king of the Jews under Roman suzerainty. The fascinating story of his reign is to be read in the works of the great, but equally worldly and calculating, Jewish historian, Josephus. It is Herod who occupies the throne when the New Testament story begins.

During all the period which followed the Babylonian

Exile a great movement, marked by no spectacular events, had been quietly going on among the Jews. This was the gradual dispersion of the nation throughout the civilized world. Palestine was a poor country and the young people, fresh, vigorous, and anxious for a better life, had emigrated in a constant stream until by New Testament times, there were far more Jews outside the Holy Land than within it. It was this worldwide diffusion of the Jewish people, the Diaspora, along with the universal use of the Greek language, which made possible the preaching journeys of St. Paul and other early Christian missionaries. Wherever they went, there were already synagogues in which they could preach and people who could understand the language which they spoke. Christians have always seen in these facts the working of God's Holy Spirit, preparing the world to receive the Gospel.

# Prophetic Books: *Proclamation of God's Justice and Mercy*

ALTHOUGH the prophetic books come last in the Old Testament, it is better to deal with them here rather than later, because they are so closely connected with the history of the nation and the greater part of them were written before the poetic books. Most of them have already been referred to in the preceding section in the proper historical order. For convenience of reference, they are considered in this section in the order in which they appear in our Bibles.

## THE NATURE OF A PROPHET

THE prophetic writings are frequently misunderstood because people think that a prophet is "one who can foretell the future" and they try to get from the prophetic books a blueprint of world history for all time to come. Only one of the so-called prophetic writings, the Book of Daniel, actually attempts to do anything of this kind, and

77

as we shall see, it is not really a prophetic book at all, in the Old Testament sense (see page 86). Although the great prophets were indeed interested in the shape of things to come, their concern was not with the remote future, but with that which lay directly before them. They could see that the events of the immediate future are always the result of what people are doing and thinking in the present.

The prophets were not fanciful visionaries who sought to disclose the secret plan of God for all subsequent history, but men of tremendously practical interests who were deeply immersed in the social, political, and moral problems of their own times. Their chief endeavor was to explain the will of God to the people of the day in which they lived and to interpret in moral terms the meaning of contemporary events. Of course they did not conceive of themselves as mere teachers or preachers, but regarded themselves quite literally as men of God, men of whom God took possession and whose minds and voices He used to declare His will. Yet, their books clearly show that they were not mere automatons, simply reproducing the words of Another. They were, rather, profoundly intelligent men who actively coöperated with God in the formulation and proclamation of His message.

A two-fold definition of a prophet will, perhaps, come somewhere near the truth. The great prophets of the eighth century and later were, on the one hand, men of outstanding intelligence and deep moral earnestness, who were in contact with all the basic forces which were stirring in their times, while on the other hand, the spirit of the living God was actually at work within them utilizing them as instruments to mould Israel according to His will.

The prophets are often difficult to understand. There are three reasons for this:

*First,* since they always spoke with regard to a particular situation, we sometimes fail to understand their meaning, because we no longer know clearly what that situation was.

*Secondly,* the addresses of the prophets were always brief and a single chapter in our Bibles today may contain several separate prophetic oracles or addresses, delivered upon different occasions and sometimes even by different men. The editors who put the prophetic books together often did not understand the material with which they were dealing any better than we do and frequently joined together oracles which are unconnected and make no particular sense when read consecutively.

*Thirdly,* since what the oracle originally referred to was often forgotten in the course of time, the true meaning of the language has sometimes been forgotten also and the words and forms have been changed as they were copied by one scribe after another until, not infrequently, passages have been corrupted to such an extent that neither the English translation nor the Hebrew original makes any very clear sense. These difficulties, of course, should not be exaggerated unduly and they should not lead us to neglect the reading of the prophetic books, because, next to the New Testament itself, they are the noblest religious writings of all time and contain some of the most stirring passages in all literature.

# ISAIAH: THE PROPHET OF FAITH IN GOD

At the head of the four so-called major[1] prophets stands the Book of Isaiah. The nucleus around which this book grew was a collection of the oracles of the eighth century Judean prophet Isaiah. Isaiah's oracles make up a large part of the first thirty-nine chapters. Isaiah exercised his ministry as a prophet in Jerusalem for more than forty years, mostly in the reigns of Ahaz and Hezekiah (see pages 62, 63), and during the successive crises of that time was the most important spiritual leader of the nation. He was possibly of noble birth since he had direct access to the ears of the king. His call to prophesy is beautifully and simply told in chapter 6. Here, in the song of the seraphim, we meet one of the great ideas in Isaiah's thought, that of the majestic and unapproachable holiness of God. To Isaiah this holiness included the thought of God's utter moral purity. The first crisis Isaiah had to meet in his prophetic ministry was that of the Syro-Ephraimite War *(Isaiah 7),* during which he first emerged as the prophet of absolute faith in God. He said, *If ye will not believe, surely ye shall not be established (Isaiah 7:9).* The same thought frequently recurs elsewhere in his teaching, as in the familiar passage, *In returning and rest shall ye be saved, in quietness and in confidence shall be your strength (Isaiah 30:15).*[2] Chapter 20 describes a later crisis of the nation's life during which the prophet walked amongst the people "naked and barefoot" for three years to try and persuade them not to join in armed revolt against

---

1 The terms major and minor are to some extent misleading and are used here only because they have become fixed in common usage.
2 See footnote, page 63.

their Assyrian overlords. The last crisis in which we know he played a part was that connected with the siege of Jerusalem by Sennacherib *(Isaiah 36-39)*. Once again Isaiah was sure that God is not on the side of the largest battalions, but of those who trust Him and do His will. When Sennacherib lifted the siege and withdrew his armies, as reported in Isaiah 37:36-38, it seemed that Isaiah's doctrine of faith had been triumphantly vindicated. Among other famous passages in the book, the most important for Christian thought are those (perhaps not by Isaiah himself) which describe the ideal future king of Israel, the Messiah *(Isaiah 9 and 11)*. *His name shall be called Wonderful, Counsellor, The mighty God, The everlasting Father, The Prince of Peace (Isaiah 9:6), and the spirit of the Lord shall rest upon him, the spirit of wisdom and understanding, the spirit of counsel and might, the spirit of knowledge and of the fear of the Lord (Isaiah 11:2)*.

### SECOND ISAIAH: THE PROPHET OF DELIVERANCE

THE second part of the book of Isaiah *(40-66)* is the work of another prophet (see page 69) or perhaps of several prophets, who lived in the days which just preceded and followed the end of the Babylonian Exile (539 B.C.), more than 150 years after the days of the eighth century Isaiah. These chapters, which are among the most familiar and appealing in the prophetic books, depict the coming glories of the kingdom of Israel and set them in striking contrast to the humiliation which the people of God have had to suffer for so long. *Comfort ye, comfort ye my people, saith your God. Speak ye comfortably to Jerusalem,*

81

*and cry unto her, that her warfare is accomplished, that her iniquity is pardoned (Isaiah 40:1, 2)*. When Christians read these chapters, they quite properly refer the promises of glory and worldwide dominion to the spiritual Israel, which is the Christian Church, rather than to the national Israel of the Jews.

Nothing in these remarkable chapters is more striking than the description in four passages *(Isaiah 42:1-4; 49:1-6; 50:4-9; 52:13–53:12)* of a mysterious and touching figure whom we call "the Suffering Servant of the Lord," an unnamed person who is to save his people, and all peoples, by suffering and death, by being wounded for their transgressions and bruised for their iniquities. Jewish interpreters were never agreed as to whom these chapters referred, but Christians have always seen in them a foreshadowing of the career of Jesus Christ and, according to the Gospels, our Lord Himself accepted them as containing the divinely intended pattern for His life. It was by the contemplation of this strange figure that He realized it was His paradoxical destiny to be a suffering Messiah.

### JEREMIAH: THE PROPHET OF THE INNER LIFE

THE second of the major prophets is JEREMIAH (see page 66) and the book which bears his name is largely composed of three kinds of literary material: oracles spoken by him and written down at his command *(see Jeremiah 36)*, autobiographical fragments in which he tells of his own life and inner thoughts *(e.g. Jeremiah 12:1-6; 20:7-18)* and biographical sections written by his faithful friend and secretary, Baruch *(e.g. Jeremiah 27, 28, 29)*. Unfortunately, the order of these materials is in great disarray, and, while the separate sections are perfectly intelligible as they stand, one needs the help of a good teacher or commentary to straighten out the sequence of events. The prophet lived through the closing years of the kingdom of Judah and was involved in all the crises of that time. He was frequently in conflict with the authorities *(e.g. Jeremiah 26)*, incurred the implacable enmity of king Jehoiakim *(Jeremiah 36:20-32)*, on more than one occasion was cast into prison and was in danger of death *(Jeremiah 20:1-6; 38:1-6; 32 and 33)*. Yet, in spite of constant opposition, he never once faltered in his declaration that Israel was doomed because it persistently rebelled against God's leadership. He warned that it was futile for Israel to resist the Babylonians since God was using them as instruments to punish His people *(e.g. Jeremiah 21:1-10)*. It may well be imagined that such defeatist talk did not make Jeremiah popular with his compatriots or their rulers. His was a lonely life for all his years of prophesying, a loneliness accentuated by his feeling that God had forbidden him to marry or take part in the normal social life of others *(Jeremiah 16:1-9)*. Only the assurance of God's constant presence made it possible for him to endure. The fine account of his call to prophesy which stands at the beginning of his book describes both his hesitation to enter upon such a life and the conviction of God-given strength which nevertheless made it possible for him to do so. Every indication is that Jeremiah was a normal, kindly, rather timid man, who loved the sights and sounds of the countryside around the little village of Anathoth which had been his home. There were many times in his career when he longed to

83

give up his unnatural life and this unpopular preaching, but always the sense of God's call and God's help spurred him onward *(Jeremiah 15:10-21)*.

One must not think of Jeremiah as a "gloomy prophet." This reputation has been given to him because of the Book of Lamentations, which he did not write. He had, it is true, a message of doom to deliver, but always behind the doom was the sense of God's great purpose which could not be frustrated, and, once the doom had taken place, Jeremiah began to speak enthusiastically and beautifully of the hope of restoration for Israel, a restoration which would, however, take place on a higher and more spiritual plane than anything the nation had previously known *(Jeremiah 32:36-44)*. In what many would consider the finest passage in the Old Testament *(Jeremiah 31:31-34)*, he speaks of the New Covenant which God would one day make with His people. The significance of this passage for Christian theology is clear when we remember the familiar words of the Communion Service, *This is my blood of the New Covenant (see St. Luke 22:20)*.

Aside from his doctrine of the New Covenant, Jeremiah's chief significance for religion is the revelation which he gives us of his own inner life of prayer and devotion. He is often called the first individual in history since he was one of the very first to record, not merely the external events in which he was concerned, but also his own inner thoughts and his private meditations *(e.g. Jeremiah 15:10-21)*. Although Jeremiah is obviously bound by some of the limitations of his age, yet he emerges from the pages of his book as one of the most human and attractive figures in all literature.

84

## EZEKIEL: THE PROPHET OF RECONSTRUCTION

THE prophet EZEKIEL is the least appealing of the major prophets, a lonely, forbidding, but towering figure among the great men of the Bible. His mind is the most difficult of them all to understand, as one must readily admit if he compares Ezekiel's verbose and fantastic account of his call to prophesy *(Ezekiel 1)* with the corresponding accounts in Isaiah 6 and Jeremiah 1. Ezekiel lived among the Jewish captives in Babylonia in the early days of the Exile and something of the awkward fancifulness of Babylonian mythology and art seems to have entered into his soul. His book is, though, more orderly than those of any of his predecessors. The first 32 chapters consist of prophecies written before the final downfall of the Hebrew kingdom (that is, between 597 and 586 B.C.). In these he plays over and over again variations on the theme, "Do not be encouraged by delusive hopes; Jerusalem is going to be totally destroyed" *(e.g. Ezekiel 4)*.

The greatest chapter among all these is the eighteenth, in which Ezekiel, incidental to his main purpose, declares that God judges men only by what they are at the moment of judgment. God does not punish an individual for the sins of his ancestors, his family, or race, nor does He punish him even for his own sins in the past if these have been sincerely repented of. God, he says, *has no pleasure in the death of the wicked (Ezekiel 18:23),* which is Ezekiel's somewhat backhanded way of saying that God loves even the sinner. Ezekiel's emphasis upon the importance of individuals represents a tremendous advance. Before his time, the Jews took it for granted that men should be dealt with in groups and that they could be held responsible for the sins of their family, their compatriots, and even of their ancestors. They believed that children would be punished for their father's sins to the third and fourth generations *(Exodus 34:7)*. How this worked out in practice can be seen by reading the horrifying story of Achan told in Joshua 7, especially verses 24, 25.

The second part of Ezekiel's book *(chapters 33-48)* consists of prophecies uttered after the final siege and destruction of Jerusalem. The prophet, who had previously spoken only of doom, here speaks almost entirely of hope, of God's plan to restore the nation in purified form under a just and humane king. The shepherds of chapter 34 are kings. The future restoration of Israel is most strikingly depicted in the remarkable vision of "the valley of dry bones" in chapter 37. The concluding chapters of the book *(40-48)* consist for the most part of laws and regulations which do not make for exciting reading, but are historically interesting as the first tentative program of life and worship to be drawn up for the reconstructed Jewish community after the Exile.

### DANIEL: THE HERALD OF THE KINGDOM OF GOD

THE fourth of the major prophets is DANIEL. This actually is not a book of prophecy at all, in the Old Testament sense of the word, and is not classified as such in the Hebrew Bible. It is an apocalypse, a kind of writing represented in the New Testament by the Book of Revelation, which uses strange, fantastic language to teach the truth that God has a plan for His world. In all the apocalypses (and there were many others besides the two which have

86

been preserved in the Bible), this plan is always described as containing certain standard elements: before the end there will be a time of great persecution, with much distress for the faithful, after which God will intervene in some striking way, destroy the heathen, and establish His rule or kingdom upon earth. Other elements are the resurrection of the dead, a judgment, and eternal happiness for the righteous. The differences among the apocalypses are due to the various ways in which they elaborate the fundamental themes. The Book of Daniel was written, as has been previously explained (see page 74), to meet a particular crisis in the history of the nation, the attempt of Antiochus Epiphanes to suppress the Jewish religion. The purpose of both parts of the book, the exciting stories about Daniel and the three Holy Children in chapters 1-6, and the apocalypse proper in chapters 7-12, is the same: to encourage the Jews to be faithful to the practice of their religion because God can be depended upon to take care of His own. One should not allow the fanciful, and often unintelligible, imagery of chapters 7-12 to blind him to the great thought which underlies them, the thought of God's dominion over the world and the realization of His purposes through the course of history.

### THE MINOR PROPHETS

In the Hebrew Bible, the rest of the prophetic writings are all part of a single volume called The Book of the Twelve. We call them minor only because their bulk is so much less than that of the major prophets, but actually such prophets as Amos and Hosea are decidedly major so far as their significance is concerned.

First in order, though not quite in order of time, is the Book of HOSEA (see page 59) who was a prophet of the northern kingdom in the days just before its final fall (721 B.C.). The burden of his preaching is that irretrievable disaster is on the way and that it is deserved because the people of Israel have preferred to worship the little gods of the Canaanite fertility religion rather than Jehovah, the god of their ancestors. Hosea, however, is known to religious history chiefly as the prophet of love, not because love was the principal thing in his message, but because he undoubtedly did conceive of God as primarily a God of love and mercy, who punished His people only as a last desperate measure and would always have been willing to forgive them if they had ever shown any sign of repentance. The first three chapters show how Hosea came to this conclusion through his own unhappy experience with a faithless wife.

JOEL is one of the latest of the prophetic books, perhaps written as late as the fourth century B.C. It begins with a description of a plague of locusts, a terrifying phenomenon which then leads the prophet on to the thought of that great "day of the Lord" which will one day come upon the world.

AMOS (see page 59) was the first of all the writing prophets, and prophesied in the northern kingdom a few years before Hosea, beginning perhaps about 750 B.C. His is one of the clearest and most virile of all the prophetic books, and is dominated by a single theme: God's demand for absolute justice in social relationships. For Amos, nothing else counts. Sacrifices, temples, worship of any kind, is meaningless unless it finds expression in a righteous social order. His thought is well summed up in the familiar quotation, *Let justice roll down as the waters, and righteousness as a mighty stream (Amos 5:24).* The famous expression *I was no prophet, neither was I a prophet's son* is an indignant denial that he was a mere prophet by profession who earned his living by telling fortunes and playing upon the religious credulity of the masses. Instead, he was a laboring man, a shepherd from Tekoa, in the kingdom of Judah, who in the midst of his work had heard God's call to be the bearer of His message to Israel *(Amos 7:14, 15; 1:1).*

Along with the great prophets whose vision was world-wide and whose interests were largely moral, we find mention of a large class of professional prophets, who were men of much smaller vision and whose message consisted largely in prophesying victory for Israel's armies and disaster for her foes. To such men as Isaiah, Jeremiah, and Ezekiel, men of this type were merely false prophets *(e.g. Ezekiel 13:1-17).* This was certainly an extreme judgment, as many of the false prophets were undoubtedly conscientious men who, rightly or wrongly, were concerned to emphasize God's favor toward His people rather than His judgment upon them. The Book of OBADIAH is an example of this kind of writing. Its subject is some terrible doom which has befallen Edom, the nation situated immediately southeast of Israel and most closely related to her by ties of kinship. Obadiah interprets her fate as an act of divine retribution for the infamous way in which the Edomites had supported the Babylonians in the days when Jerusalem was destroyed.

The Book of JONAH represents as broad and generous a

point of view as is to be found anywhere in the Old Testament. It is, as a matter of fact, not a book of prophecy, but a story about a prophet, a little novel which is intended to show how ridiculous the attitude of the narrow-minded nationalist really is. Jonah, the legendary prophet who is the central figure of the book, is intended to be typical of those Jews of the author's time (the late post-exilic period) who felt that God had no concern with anyone except themselves. The point of the book is that God in His universal love cares as much for the people of Nineveh as for them. The so-called whale, really "a great fish," is merely a bit of picturesque detail which the author introduces in order to make his story more colorful and interesting.

The Book of MICAH is one of the greatest of the minor prophetic books, although the work of the eighth century Judean prophet Micah, a younger contemporary of Isaiah (see page 64), occupies only the first three chapters. His message is essentially the same as that of Amos—God's demand for justice in social relations. The anonymous remainder of the book *(chapters 4-7)* contains the beautiful picture of the Jerusalem of the future situated in quiet beauty as the spiritual center of a world at peace *(chapter 4:1-5; found in part also in Isaiah 2)*. Here also is to be found that definition of God's demands upon man which is the best of all summaries of the content and spirit of Old Testament religion: *What doth the Lord require of thee, but to do justly and to love kindness and to walk humbly with thy God (Micah 6:8).*

NAHUM, like Obadiah, is a representative of the nationalistic type of prophecy. The entire content of the book is a savage exultation over the fall of Nineveh the capital of the great Assyrian Empire (612 B.C.). Regarded purely as literature, it is one of the most stirring poems in the Hebrew language and like the Book of Obadiah vividly pictures the consequences of national pride and cruelty.

The prophet HABAKKUK (see page 68) lived during the days when the new Babylonian Empire was sweeping everything aside in its triumphal progress. The problem with which the main part of the book deals is the perennial one of attempting to reconcile the apparent prosperity of the wicked with the conviction that a just and omnipotent God is in control of the forces of nature and history *(Habakkuk 1:13)*. Habakkuk finds no satisfying intellectual answer, but concludes that the righteous man will nevertheless find the path of life by holding steadfastly to God and the practices of his religion: *The righteous shall live by his faith (Habakkuk 2:4)*.

ZEPHANIAH (see page 66) attempted to interpret prophetically the situation apparently created by the incursion of the Scythian barbarians into the Near East in the late seventh century B.C. The great medieval Christian hymn *Dies irae* (468 in the 1940 Hymnal) is based upon Zephaniah's description of the coming Day of the Lord *(note especially Zephaniah 1:15)*.

HAGGAI (see page 70), who delivered the four brief oracles now contained in his book within a few weeks toward the end of the year 520 B.C., had only one concern, that the Jews should immediately begin the rebuilding of the Temple which the Babylonians had destroyed in 586 B.C. He explains that all the distress which has come upon them since their return from Exile is due to their neglect of this great task.

ZECHARIAH (see page 70) was active at the same time as Haggai and in the same cause. He, however, had broader interests, shows much of the moral seriousness of the older prophets *(e.g. Zechariah 7:8-14)* and, in chapter 8, draws one of the most appealing pictures to be found in the Old Testament of life in the wonderfully restored Jerusalem of the future. Much of Zechariah's message is surrounded by fanciful imagery which is similar to that of the later apocalyptic writers. The last chapters of his book *(9-14)* were written by another and much later hand, or by several other hands. The material which they contain is partly apocalyptical in character and is very difficult to interpret. The most familiar passage is that which describes the peaceful coming of the messianic king: *Behold, thy king cometh unto thee; he is just and having salvation; lowly, and riding upon an ass, and upon a colt the foal of an ass (9:9).*

The last book in the Old Testament is MALACHI (see page 72). It is actually anonymous, since the word *Malachi* is not a proper name, but merely the word in 3:1 which is translated *my messenger.* The unknown author of the oracles contained in it lived in the time shortly before the coming of Nehemiah and Ezra and describes the low spiritual state of the people, particularly as regards their neglect of the worship of God *(Malachi 1:7)* and the prevalence of divorce among them *(Malachi 2:14).*

# Poetical and Wisdom Books:
# *Meditations on God and Life*

THE books to be discussed here (Job through the Song of Solomon) all belong in the third section of the Hebrew Bible, *the Writings,* as do also some of the books previously discussed, *e.g.* Ruth, Daniel, I-II Chronicles, etc., and were regarded by the Jews as on a somewhat lower level of inspiration and importance than the Law and the Prophets. In general, they all belong to the later period of Old Testament history and are, indeed, with the possible exception of some of the Psalms, all post-Exilic. Although the Authorized (King James) Version prints these books as prose, they are all, with the exception of Ecclesiastes, written in poetic form, as the Revised Version clearly indicates. Hebrew poetry has no scheme of rhymes, nor does it have precisely measured syllabic feet as does English poetry, but it does have very strongly marked rhythmic patterns. Its most striking characteristic is parallelism, as one can see by observing the asterisks which, in the Prayer Book version of the Psalms, always divide the Psalm-verse into two nearly equal halves. The second half is always parallel in some way to the first. It usually expresses the same thought in different words, but sometimes gives a contrasting or complementary thought. In Hebrew poetry, as in other poetic literatures, the language and vocabulary are more elevated than in prose.

### JOB: WHY DO THE INNOCENT SUFFER?

THE Book of JOB is not only a great work of the poetic imagination, but also a profound discussion of one of the most difficult of religious questions, *Why does God permit the innocent to suffer?* Instead of approaching the question in an abstract way, the author adopted the form of drama, though it was not, of course, actually intended for stage production, since the Hebrews had no theater. He selected for his hero an ideally righteous man, Job, who was visited by a series of almost unendurable calamities. He then represents Job as disputing with three of his friends, Eliphaz, Bildad, and Zophar, as to the justice of his fate. The friends represent the old-fashioned, orthodox point of view which regarded all misfortune as punishment for sin. They insist that, since Job suffers so much, he must be a very bad man. Job, conscious of his own rectitude, though not in any smug or self-satisfied way, insists that such is not the case and that a God who can permit such things to happen is not truly a just God *(Job 9:22-24; 19:6-9)*. He demands that he be permitted to confront God and hear how God would justify His ways *(Job 23:3-5)*. While there has been much discussion as to precisely what answer the author of Job intended to give to the question

94

with which he began, he at least seems to say that no completely adequate solution is possible for the human mind. What men need to satisfy their eager and anxious souls, he seems to say, is not intellectual answers to their difficult questions, but the actual personal experience of God *(Job 38:1ff; 40:1-5).*

The first two chapters and the last chapter of the book are in prose and are written in a very different mood from the poem. They seem to contain an old folk tale which the author of the poem has merely taken as a convenient framework for his magnificent picture of the agony of a human soul. Both in Hebrew and English much of the language of the book is difficult to understand and there are a number of intrusions and disarrangements in the various sections which confuse the main outline of argument and development. Nevertheless, it can safely be said that, in spite of its length and difficulty, there is no Old Testament book which has more to disclose with repeated readings.

### THE PSALTER: PRAISING GOD IN SONG

THE Book of PSALMS is a hymn book, a collection of religious lyrics of many different types and moods which were used in the Temple at Jerusalem to accompany public worship. A careful reading of the Psalms even in English reveals the fact that they were written by men of varied interests and diversified situation. Tradition ascribes the Psalms to David, but many of them are explicitly ascribed in their titles to other persons *(e.g. 73, 89, 90),* and it is doubtful if the great King of Israel was actually responsible for any of them. The titles, which profess to name the author and describe the situation in which the Psalm was written *(e.g. 34)*, are much later than the Psalms themselves and were added by editors who were in no better position than we are to discuss such things. We shall do well simply to accept the fact that the Psalms, like the hymns in the Hymnal, were written by many different authors, whose names have long been forgotten. Many of the Psalms are certainly of post-Exilic origin and the collection as a whole was made for use in the second Temple, that of Zerubbabel (see page 70). Nowhere in the Old Testament do we come so close to the heart of its religion as in these inspired songs, which are, for the most part, direct expressions of the faith and piety of the men of ancient Israel.

A brief list will show by way of a few examples how rich is the variety of material contained in the Psalter: Moral instruction, 1, 15; an evening prayer, 4; hymns of praise to God in nature, 8, 19, 29, 104; a song of personal trust, 23; a processional hymn, 24; meditations on the problem of injustice in the world, 37, 73; a royal marriage hymn, 45; hymn to God as saviour, 46; a confession of sins, 51; a prayer for the king, 72; a lament in time of national misfortune, 79; hymns for pilgrims, 84, 121, 122; a lament by one who longs to make the pilgrimage to Jerusalem, 42, 43; a hymn in praise of the Holy City, 87; solemn meditation upon the shortness of human life, 90; praise to God as king, 95-99; praise to God for His love and kindness, 103; solemn public thanksgiving, 107, 136; an acrostic (an artificial poem each part of which begins with a successive letter of the Hebrew alphabet), 119; a meditation on brotherly love, 133; a meditation on God's omniscience and omnipresence, 139.

This list is far from complete, either as regards categories or examples, but will serve to indicate why Jewish and Christian people of every age have always been able to find in the Psalter poetry which could express their every mood. A few of the Psalms belong to an outgrown stage of man's religious thought and are rarely used in public worship. These are the so-called imprecatory Psalms (such as 58 and 109), and, when they are used in Christian worship, are interpreted as referring to spiritual and not personal enemies.

### PROVERBS: THOUGHTS ON HOW TO LIVE WISELY

THE Book of PROVERBS is not a collection of folk sayings, as the title might lead one to suppose. The brief moral apothegms which make up most of the book are highly polished literary maxims, the product of professional teachers (wise men) who used them for the practical purpose of teaching the good life to their pupils, mostly young men of the upper classes. Like the Psalms, most of the Proverbs are late, and the ascription of them to Solomon *(1:1)* is a harmless literary device common to the age in which they arose.[1] This book has often been criticized as presenting a philosophy of enlightened self-interest as a substitute for the high ethical idealism of the prophets. This is to misunderstand its purpose which is a purely practical one. It does not deal with morality on the level of profound religious insight, but for the most part attempts merely to commend the ordinary decencies of civ-

---

[1] Thus, a book of philosophy in the Apocrypha, written in Greek, is called the Wisdom of Solomon, and two books written even later were called, respectively, the Psalms and the Odes of Solomon.

ilized existence to young men who were about to enter the fields of diplomacy and commerce. The morality it teaches is earthly and common sense. Even here, though, there are ethical precepts which rise above this level, such as *If thine enemy be hungry, give him bread to eat; and if he be thirsty, give him water to drink (Proverbs 25:21).* The thinking of the wise men, also, occasionally led them into deeper speculations than usual, as in the beautiful discussion of the role played by Wisdom in the creation of the world *(Proverbs 8:22-36)* a passage which clearly forms part of the background to the first chapter of the fourth Gospel, *In the beginning was the Word (St. John 1:1).*

### ECCLESIASTES: THE VOICE OF DISILLUSIONMENT

THE Book of ECCLESIASTES shows another direction in which the thought of the wise men sometimes took them. The endeavor to find a rational and common sense basis for morality could, and did, lead some of them to negative and skeptical conclusions, just as, in the modern world, the attempt to base morality on something other than religion often leads to moral cynicism as well as religious disbelief. This book was written by a thoroughly disillusioned man, who had tried everything and found no satisfaction in anything. He rejected the idea that a moral life is practically advantageous since, so far as he could see, the good and the bad come alike to a wretched end *(Ecclesiastes 9:2; 11).* He did not doubt the existence of God, but saw little evidence that God is concerned with man. He deprecated too much attention to the practices of religion *(Ecclesiastes 5:1-6; 7:16).* His positive conclusion is that one should strive to live the simple life *(Ecclesiastes 5:18-*

*20)* and practice the golden mean *(Ecclesiastes 7:16).* Ecclesiastes could hardly have been included in the Canon
of Scripture if the author had not chosen to write under
the pseudonym of Solomon and the book had not later
been given an orthodox coloring by the addition of verses
here and there which provide an antidote to the prevail-
ing skepticism *(e.g. Ecclesiastes 2:26; 8:11-13; 12:13, 14).*
Nevertheless, this is an extremely valuable book since it
exposes the inadequacy of all attempts to create a satisfying view of life on the basis of mere intellectual speculation without regard to historic religious faith. The gloomy
rationalistic pessimism of Ecclesiastes is an excellent foil
for the religious, though intensely realistic, optimism of
the Christian Gospel.

#### SOLOMON'S SONG: THE BEAUTY OF HUMAN LOVE

THE SONG OF SOLOMON, the third of the Biblical books at-
tributed to the great king of Israel's golden age, is actually
a collection of Hebrew love lyrics, compiled perhaps to be
sung at a wedding celebration. They are notable for their
exuberant oriental imagery and for their unusual feeling
for the beauties of nature *(e.g. The Song of Solomon 2:10-
13).* They came to have a religious significance only after
they were reinterpreted to refer, not to the love of a
man for a maid, but to God's love for his people Israel.
When the Old Testament became a part of the Christian
Bible, the book was understood to refer to Christ's love for
the Church, as one can see by referring to the chapter
headings in the Authorized Version. This is, of course,
poetic license and is perfectly legitimate so long as we do
not suppose it was the purpose of the original writer.

# Religious Faith and Practice in the Old Testament

While the Old Testament contains many books and they represent many different interests and points of view, yet there are certain basic convictions about God and the meaning of life which are common to most of them. It is this underlying unity of viewpoint which justifies speaking of the religion, or theology, of the Old Testament. Beside this basic unity of faith, the people of ancient Israel were bound together also in a unity of worship and religious observance which, especially in later times, tended to make of them not merely a Nation, but a spiritual community, a Church.

## THE OLD TESTAMENT IDEA OF GOD

The most distinctive doctrine of the Old Testament with regard to God is that He is One. The basic creed of Judaism to the present day is *Hear, O Israel: the Lord thy God is one Lord (Deuteronomy 6:4)*. In the earliest times, this doctrine seems to have meant that there was only one God for Israel, but later on it came to mean that only one God exists and that there is no other God beside Him. This true monotheism finds its most beautiful expression in certain passages in Second Isaiah *(e.g. Isaiah 44:6; see page 81)*. According to the developed thought of Israel, this God was the Creator of everything in heaven and earth *(Genesis 1)* and constantly sustains everything by His love and power *(Psalm 104)*. Although God is often associated with the forces of nature, He is never identified with them, as is done in most pagan religions and in much modern religious thought. God is always represented as superior to nature and in control of it *(Psalm 18:7-15; I Kings 19:11, 12)*.

God in the Old Testament is always represented as personal, never as an impersonal force. So intense is His personality that He even has a personal name, Jehovah or Yahweh *(Exodus 6:2, 3)*; usually translated in our English versions by *the Lord*. He is often described as acting like a man—loving, angry, repentant, speaking, even smelling and sleeping. In very early times these expressions may have been understood literally, but in later times they were merely poetic ways of referring to His activity, since no other language was available. The Hebrews felt it was more reverent to use even the most extremely human (anthropomorphic) language about God than to use the abstract language of philosophy. Philosophy tends to make God merely the object of our speculative thought rather than the living God who reigns as King over His creation, directs the course of history to His own great ends, and demands personal loyalty from His creatures.

Along with this emphasis upon His personality, the Old Testament also insists that God is spiritual. Although it is necessary to use human language if one is to speak of Him at all, yet God is not man and the difference between the two is an infinite one *(Numbers 23:19; Isaiah 55:8, 9)*. In order to safeguard the spirituality of God, the men of the Old Testament were forbidden to make any visible image or representation of Him *(Exodus 20:4)* and the prophets heaped bitter scorn on those who worshipped idols *(Isaiah 44:9-20)*. While the Old Testament does not speculate as to what God's nature is, yet it plainly implies that, in contrast to man and all other creatures, *God is Spirit (Isaiah 31:1-3)*.

Finally, the Old Testament declares that God is a righteous God. He does not operate by caprice, but according to the fixed and unchangeable law of His own being *(I Samuel 15:29; Genesis 18:25; Psalm 146)*. Because He is righteous, He demands righteousness from His worshippers. No worship is pleasing to Him which is not an expression of a life lived in obedience to His ethical demands *(Amos 5:21-24; Isaiah 58:1-12)*. Thus at the heart of the Old Testament is the finest moral teaching known to mankind before the coming of Jesus Christ, a moral teaching which is neither primarily negative or individualistic, but which is positive and above all is concerned with justice and decency in social relations *(see, for example, Deuteronomy 5:7-21; Leviticus 19:11-18; Psalm 15; Job 31)*.

Although the Unity of God is one of the basic doctrines of the Old Testament, yet there are also to be found there certain ideas which can be regarded as intimations of that richer and more adequate conception of God which is expressed in the Christian doctrine of the Trinity within the Divine Unity. The Old Testament frequently speaks of the Spirit by which God's power becomes operative in the world. Sometimes, especially in the earlier period, this was conceived crudely as a mere physical force *(Judges 14:6; II Kings 2:16)*, but later was associated chiefly with spiritual endowments such as the gift of prophecy *(Ezekiel 2:1)* and with ethical guidance *(Psalm 51:11)*. In one passage, the Spirit is spoken of in terms which imply personality *(Isaiah 63:10)*. The Old Testament also speaks of God as working by means of His word, as in creation *(Genesis 1, cf. Psalm 33:6)* and in the book of Proverbs *(8:22-30)* a similar role is given to Wisdom. These conceptions are developed and their implications more fully realized in the Christian doctrine of God.

### THE OLD TESTAMENT IDEA OF MAN

ACCORDING to the Old Testament, man was created by God "in His own image" *(Genesis 1:27)*. Therefore man is different from all the rest of creation. Man was created to be happy and to enjoy fellowship with God, but was given free will so that he could choose whether he would live in obedience and voluntary fellowship with Him or not. Since Man disobeyed and chose to follow his own will rather than God's, misery and death came to rule in the world and Man's lot became desperately unhappy *(Genesis 3)*. He is, therefore, not merely God's creature, but a fallen creature who is in need of divine assistance to save him from the tragic situation which is the result of his sin. Since God is a Father who loves His children *(Psalm*

103

*103:13)* and does not wish them to perish even though they have rebelled against Him, it was always His ultimate purpose to redeem men from the slavery which they had created for themselves *(Psalm 130:7, 8).*

In the Old Testament story of creation, God says, *It is not good that man should be alone (Genesis 2:18).* All through the Old Testament (and also the New) there is this sense that man is in his nature a social being. He always is seen as part of some larger group, the family, the clan, or the tribe. The individual is so closely related to this group that he is often punished or rewarded simply because he belongs to it, and not because of his own personal merits or demerits *(e.g. Joshua 7:24, 25; Exodus 20:5).* In its extreme form this emphasis upon "the solidarity of the group" is repugnant to our Christian conscience and the worst features of it were finally repudiated by the prophet Ezekiel *(see page 85).* In its best form this doctrine embodies a very important truth about human nature and remains a constant feature of Old Testament religion. Man does not fully realize his nature when he lives to himself alone. He is a human being in the complete sense of the word only when he lives in society, fully participating in the give-and-take of social intercourse and coöperating with others for common ends. Because the Hebrews felt this so keenly they never pictured salvation as a merely individual matter; man must find his individual salvation within the redeemed community. In the Old Testament the community within which men find the abundant life is the nation of Israel; in the New Testament, of course, it is the Christian Church.

## THE IDEA OF THE COVENANT

BASIC to the religion of the Old Testament (and of the New) is the idea that the relation of God to His people is founded upon a covenant. The very name we give to the two parts of the Bible shows the importance of this idea, for though we call them the Old and New Testaments, yet the word translated Testament really means Covenant and is so rendered on the title page of the revised versions. The word thus translated meant in its original sense a solemn agreement and was used by the men of the Old Testament for many different kinds of agreements which men entered into in order to regulate their life together. Treaties, contracts, partnerships, all relationships which involved mutual privileges and responsibilities, were embodied in covenants.

According to the Bible, when God saved the tribes of Israel out of the land of Egypt and created Israel as a nation, He entered into a covenant with them by which He promised to be their God, if they would promise to trust in Him and do His will *(Exodus 19:5; 24:1-8)*. God's part of the covenant was to be a King and Father to His people, to protect them and deliver them from trouble; the people's part was to live in accordance with the just and holy laws which God had given them. Thus, for the Old Israel, the covenant was based primarily upon written laws, or, as the Hebrews themselves would have said, the Law *(Torah)*, meaning by that chiefly the first five books of the Bible.

Although the Old Covenant was based upon laws, yet we must be on our guard against conceiving of it in too narrowly legalistic a fashion. The whole conception of covenant among the Hebrews had a broader meaning than our definition of it as a solemn agreement might seem to suggest. While the Hebrews used the word for any kind of formal agreement between two individuals, groups, or nations, yet they also used it for all kinds of relationships in which there was no thought of bargaining or of entering into an explicit legal contract. In Hebrew thought there was a covenant implicit in every special relationship into which men might enter: between a husband and his wife, between a man and his friend, between a nation and its king. Thus, for the Hebrew, the basic connotation of the word covenant was not so much that of legal responsibility as of personal and affectionate relationship. Wherever a new relationship arose between persons, there a covenant came into being and certain duties and privileges were involved on both sides. So when God chose to take Israel for His own people, the very creation of such a relationship, for the Hebrew mind, involved the establishment of a covenant. When the men of the Old Testament thought of this covenant, the first idea which naturally came to their minds was that of the wonderful love and condescension of God which made Him wish to enter into such a personal relationship with men. The covenant, for them, was not a legal enactment, but an expression of God's mercy and a pledge of divine grace.

There would naturally be a tendency among unimaginative people to lay undue stress upon the external aspects of the covenant and to feel that man had discharged his duties sufficiently when he merely conformed to the divine Law in a mechanical way without feeling any sense of personal dependence upon God. For this reason a covenant in which written and codified law played so large a part eventually had to give way to a higher form of covenant, just as the relationship which is natural between a young child and its father must sometime give way to a more mature form of relationship. Just before the Exile, when the whole basis of national life among the Hebrews was being destroyed, the prophet Jeremiah looked into the future and prophesied that the day would come when God would establish a new covenant with His people, based upon surer foundations, upon laws written in men's hearts rather than upon tables of stone *(Jeremiah 31:31)*. Our Lord fulfilled this prophecy and told His disciples on the night before He died that the shedding of His blood would actually establish this new covenant *(St. Luke 22:20)*. Because we believe He did this, we call the collection of books which describe His work and its immediate consequences The New Covenant or New Testament.

As Christians, then, we too are in a covenant relationship with God. This means that our relationship with Him is not a formless, indefinite thing, dependent upon our whims and feelings or upon God's caprice. God is always the same and our relationship with Him is based upon principles which do not change. God has promised His grace and help and we have promised obedience. This is another way of saying that, from the human side, our relationship with God is a moral relationship. It does not depend upon emotion or upon our doing merely what seems right to us at the moment. The only possible relationship we can have with God is that which arises out of a sincere effort to discover what His will is and to obey

Him whole-heartedly. The conception of religion as a covenant relationship to God removes it entirely from all sentimentality and vagueness and sets it firmly in the sphere of moral obedience. It is God who makes the first move to establish the relationship and who must ultimately sustain it; but men must sustain it too by responding in love and loyalty.

The basic requirement of God under the Old Covenant, established by the redemption of His people out of Egypt, was careful observance of His laws; under the New Covenant, established by the redemption of mankind through the Cross, the basic requirement is faith in Jesus Christ. Under both covenants what God really asks of men is not merely external conformity to conditions arbitrarily imposed, but glad and loyal acceptance of a gift of grace which has been freely offered.

### THE FUTURE LIFE

WHILE the ancient Hebrews certainly believed in some kind of survival after death, they had no hope of a happy immortality until the very latest period of Old Testament history. Except for a few favored souls such as Enoch and Elijah, life beyond the grave (in *Sheol*) was conceived as a wraithlike existence which hardly deserved the name of life at all *(Psalm 88:5, 11, 12)*. Thus all rewards, satisfactions, and punishments were conceived as being given in the present life *(Deuteronomy 28:1-23; Psalm 37; Proverbs 13:21, 22)*. Obviously, such a view as this is not in accord with the realities of life and eventually gave rise to grave difficulties in the minds of thoughtful men such as the authors of the Book of Job and Psalm 73. The wicked often seem to prosper and the good to suffer in this life. We can see at various places in this later period that the Hebrews were reaching out toward the idea of a future life as a partial answer to the problem of reconciling a belief in God's justice with the evident injustice of life in this world *(Job 14:7-15; Psalm 16:10, 11)*, but the doctrine is clearly stated only in two of the latest passages in the Old Testament, Daniel 12:2, 3 and Isaiah 26:19.[1] In both these places, the idea of the future life takes the form of a belief in the resurrection of the body, rather than a natural immortality of the soul, since, unlike the Greeks, the Hebrews did not think of man as being made up of a body and a soul, but conceived of him as an indivisible unity, neither part of which could exist without the other. It is this doctrine of the future life which is also taught in the New Testament and in the creeds, *I believe in the resurrection of the body.*

### THE LAW AND ITS OBSERVANCES

THE first five books of the Old Testament are called the Law, and contain a great many regulations both of a moral and ceremonial character, especially the books of Leviticus, Numbers, and Deuteronomy. For the Christian these are the least interesting and least profitable parts of the Bible. That is partly because, in general, laws do not make very interesting reading, but also because these particular laws are now for the most part of merely antiquarian concern, since the whole system of religion under law was abrogated by the Christian Gospel. It is the special service of St. Paul to have shown that the Law has no

---

[1] A passage which comes from a much later writer than the eighth century prophet Isaiah.

longer any claim upon Christians *(Galatians 2:16)*. We must be careful, however, not to underestimate the value and importance of law in the development of man's religious life. Even Paul says that *the law is holy, and the commandment holy and righteous and good (Romans 7:12)*. Before men can live under grace they must learn to live under law; just as a child must first be trained under a discipline of rules and regulations before it can be trusted to make free use of its God-given liberty. So the laws which form the basis of the covenant in the Old Testament represent a necessary step in the education of man in preparation for the covenant of grace which was established in Jesus Christ. As Paul says, *The Law was our custodian until Christ came (Galatians 3:24 RSV)*.

Many of the laws are of a moral nature and are permanently valid, as setting forth minimum norms of conduct. Others, even some of a moral nature, are definitely outmoded and still others have been explicitly altered by our Lord's command *(St. Matthew 5:20-48)*. The Christian tests them all by the final standard, the mind of Christ.

### SACRIFICE

THE greater part of the laws of the Pentateuch are of a ceremonial nature and have no longer any validity for the Christian. We cannot, however, simply ignore them, since the New Testament presupposes a knowledge of many of their more important provisions, especially those which have to do with the offering of sacrifice. To the Jews of post-Exilic times, the whole elaborate ritual of sacrifice was part of a sacramental system which God had ordained for the purpose of enabling man to remain in a state of fellowship with Him. The men of the Old Testament did not believe that sacrifice by itself had power to obtain forgiveness of sin. Only contrition and amendment of life could do that. But the sacrifices were believed to be the means God had provided to remove the taint which remained even after sin was forgiven. An expression constantly used is *to make atonement for (e.g. Leviticus 1:4)*, and the sense of it is probably, "to cover over or blot out" the unwholesome effects of sin, which would otherwise exclude one from full communion with God. The philosophy which was used to explain the efficacy of sacrifice is a somewhat complex and obscure one, based in large part upon a belief in the mysterious potency of blood *(Leviticus 17:11)*. For our purpose it is sufficient simply to state that the basic reason for observing the intricate rules and regulations provided in Leviticus 1-7 was not that these things had any magical virtue, but simply that God had willed it so. Therefore, the meticulous observance of the Law's provisions with respect to these things was a symbol of one's complete and whole-hearted obedience to God's will. Unfortunately, this noble view could easily be corrupted. Unimaginative people could suppose that the rites had value in themselves, and might become more concerned with the careful observance of the rules than with the spirit which lay back of them. This could easily happen with regard to any provision of the Law, and that it did happen is shown in St. Matthew 23:23.

## OTHER ESTABLISHED RITES: THE CHURCH CALENDAR

APART from the regular sacrifices, the principal rites of Old Testament religion were these:

Circumcision was a rite, corresponding somewhat to Christian baptism, by which the Hebrew child was initiated into the covenant community *(Genesis 17)*.

Then there were the various solemn observances of the year, above all the regular weekly Sabbath, the seventh day of the week, on which no labor was to be performed *(Deuteronomy 5:12)*.

The New Year's day differed in different periods, but according to one calendar at any rate, the year began in the month Nisan or Abib (approximately our April) and the first great feast was the Passover which also included the Feast of Unleavened Bread, commemorating the Exodus from Egypt *(Exodus 12; Deuteronomy 16:1-7)*.

Fifty days later came the Feast of Pentecost, originally a festival of the grain harvest, but later observed in honor of the giving of the Law *(Deuteronomy 16:9-12)*.

In the fall, when, according to the system now in use by the Jews, the New Year began, came the Day of Atonement, Yom Kippur *(Leviticus 16)*, the most solemn day of all, when the high priest entered the inner sanctuary of the Temple, the Holy of Holies and made atonement for all the sins which the people had committed throughout the year. The most interesting part of the ceremony was that of driving out the scapegoat which was believed to carry the sins of the people away into the desert *(Leviticus 16:20-22)*.

Later in the same month *(Tishri)* came the Feast of Tabernacles, the great harvest festival, also observed in later times as a commemoration of the dwelling in tabernacles or booths during the wilderness wanderings *(Deuteronomy 16:13-17)*.

The Feasts of Purim (March) and Hanukkah (December), which are important observances in later Judaism, were established long after the Law was compiled. The book of Esther *(9:26-32)* describes the founding of Purim and I Maccabees *(4:59)* that of Hanukkah.

## THE TEMPLE

THE sacrificial worship of the Hebrews centered in the Temple at Jerusalem and after 621 B.C. (page 65) was permitted nowhere else. The Temple of Solomon and its furnishings are described in II Kings 6 and 7 and much can also be learned about it from the account given of the Tabernacle which the nomadic Hebrews were believed to have carried about with them in the wilderness *(Exodus 25-30)*. The Temple was not a building for worship, like a church or synagogue, but was believed in some real way to be the "House" of God. Worship and sacrifice took place at the altar in the great open court in front of the temple. The Temple itself was divided into two rooms: the Holy Place and the Holiest Place. Only the priests went into the Holy Place, which contained the Table of Shewbread, the great seven-branched lampstand, and the golden altar of incense. Back of the Holy Place was the Holiest Place (Holy of Holies), into which only the high priest went, once in the year, on the Day of Atonement. This contained the figures of the winged cherubim and the Ark of the Covenant, a great chest above which God's Presence was believed mysteriously to dwell. There were three temples altogether in Hebrew history, the Temple of Solomon, the Temple of Zerubbabel, and finally the Great Temple built by Herod the Great which was still standing in our Lord's day *(e.g. St. John 2:19, 20)*. The general features of all these temples were the same. The priesthood which presided over the worship of the temple was strictly hereditary and all its members were believed to be descendants of Aaron, the brother of Moses.

Christ brought this whole elaborate scheme of worship and sacrifice to an end, and much of the New Testament is devoted to showing how His life, death, and resurrection completely and finally accomplished the great work of atonement and reconciliation for which the religion of the Law was only a preparation and foreshadowing. This is especially the theme of Galatians, Romans, and the epistle to the Hebrews.

### ISRAEL'S HOPE: THE MESSIAH

THE religion of the Old Testament, particularly in the later period, was a forward-looking religion. Recognizing fully the prevalence of sin and suffering in the world as at present constituted, the Hebrews looked with inextinguishable hope for a new mighty act of God which would restore the world to the perfection which its Creator intended and bring man back into fellowship with God and into harmony with His purposes. The worse the external situation became, the more brightly this hope shone. It became an integral article of Jewish faith that God would one day intervene in the natural course of history and establish His perfect rule (the Kingdom of God) upon earth. There would be peace and brotherhood among all men in a miraculously renovated universe. Typical expressions of this hope are to be found in Micah 4:1-5; Isaiah 65:17-25; Jeremiah 31:31-34. Sometimes the Old Testament writers speak as though God's kingdom would be established by Himself alone, without the aid of any intermediary, but in other passages there is the expectation of a king of the line of David, a perfect ruler, who will be God's agent in the building of the new order as in Isaiah 9:2-7; 11:1-9; Micah 5:2-4; Jeremiah 23:5-8; Ezekiel 34:23-24. This figure of the glorious future king attained more definite form as time went on and in the period after the Old Testament he came to be called the Messiah.[2] Under oppression by foreign powers, as for instance the days of the Roman Empire, the expectation of the Messiah became especially acute. We are, of course, aware of this from a reading of the New Testament.

In addition to the figure of the Messianic King of David's line, two other figures in the Old Testament are associated with Israel's hope for the future. One is the so-called Suffering Servant who appears in certain parts of the work of II Isaiah (see page 81) especially chapter 52:13–53:12. This figure probably symbolized originally the suffering people of Israel, but he is described in such vivid terms that one can hardly help thinking of him as an individual. Indeed, various students have attempted at times to identify him with some well-known tragic figure in Old Testament history. He is described as one who is gentle and kind *(Isaiah 42:3)*, whose mission is to bring light to the Gentile world *(Isaiah 49:6)* but in the pursuit of his task is despised by mankind as an ugly and

---

[2] The term itself means merely the anointed one and, as a common noun is found in many places in the Old Testament. It is one of the usual titles of the king *(e.g. I Samuel 24:6)* since anointing was the ceremony by which the king was inducted into office. The term was literally translated in the Greek Bible by the corresponding Greek word *Christ*.

contemptible person *(Isaiah 53:1-3)*. He dies for the sins of others and offers his life as a sacrifice to God *(Isaiah 53:4-6, 10)*, but at last is victorious over his sufferings and is exalted to high honor *(Isaiah 53:10-12)*. The Suffering Servant is a very different figure from the glorious future king and he does not seem usually to have been identified with him.

The third figure is that described in Daniel *(7:13)* as *one like unto a son of man,* meaning, in the Semitic idiom, merely "one like a man." He, too, originally was a symbol of the Jewish people and the meaning of the chapter is that the last great kingdom in history will be the Kingdom of God and His faithful people Israel. This figure also was in time individualized. In a later period there came to be certain circles which definitely expected that the Kingdom of God would be established through the agency of a glorious figure, the Son of Man, whose place was by the throne of God, but who would one day come on the clouds of heaven to bring in the new order which God had ordained.

It is in this great hope of Israel that the direct link between the Old Testament and the New is to be found. In Jesus Christ all the hopes of Israel were realized, for He was the expected Messiah, not a worldly and political Messiah, but a Messiah in whom were gathered up into one consistent pattern all the fragmentary visions of the seers of ancient times, One who was at the same time the Son of David, the Son of Man, and the Suffering Servant of the Lord.

*The Lord*
*Is Come*

PART THREE

The New Testament

# The Four Gospels: *Records of Jesus' Earthly Life*

THE New Testament relates the two con-
cluding and climactic episodes of the great story begun in
the Old Testament. There is, first of all, the account of
the life, death, and resurrection of Jesus Christ in whom
were fulfilled the hopes and dreams of the Old Israel. This
is the story told in the four Gospels. Secondly, there is
the story of that broadening of the stream of life of the
Old Israel which resulted in the establishment of the New
Israel, the Christian Church. It is this which is told in the
Book of Acts and in the Epistles. Both these events had
been clearly foreshadowed in the Old Testament, the first
in the eager certainty of the great prophets that God
would one day act decisively for the redemption of His
people through One who would be their Prophet, Priest,
and King; the second in the noble speculations concerning the ultimate mission of Israel to all mankind, found
especially in the Second Isaiah and his pupils.

IF the story of the New Testament were to be told in the order in which its books were written, it would begin with the Epistles of St. Paul, for all these were written before any of the Gospels. St. Paul was dead before even Mark, the first of the Gospels, was put into shape. While it does not appear practical to begin the study of the New Testament in this way, it should always be remembered that the earliest Christians had no Gospels such as ours and their faith was based upon the kind of preaching and teaching which are illustrated in the Pauline letters. What they knew of Jesus Christ was what they were told by such men as Paul and the Twelve, whose testimony was based either upon a personal knowledge of our Lord's earthly life, as in the case of the Twelve, or upon a vivid and equally personal experience of His risen life, as in the case of Paul. It was only after most of these men were dead and the day of the eye-witnesses was drawing to a close that it seemed wise to set down their testimony in the form of gospels which should tell, in consecutive form, the story which the apostolic teachers told only in a broken and fragmentary way.

The earliest preachers of the Gospel, both the apostles and those who at second-hand repeated their message, were not much concerned to give their hearers a complete biography of Jesus Christ. They concentrated their attention primarily on certain major events in His career, especially His death and the triumph over death which was the unmistakable sign that God had set the seal of His favor upon Him. Thus it came about that the earliest part of the Gospel story to take shape was an account of our Lord's suffering, death, and resurrection. As regards His teaching and the other events of His life, there seems to have been no particular attempt to preserve them in their original setting or sequence. His sayings and parables and familiar stories about Him were used by the apostolic preachers as texts or illustrations for discourses on their favorite themes, and the form which many of them have in the Gospels today still reveals the original use to which they were put. As a result, the different Gospels often preserve the sayings of Jesus and the events of His life in widely different contexts and often with internal differences which point to the use made of them in preaching and teaching before they were ever set down in writing.

We must, therefore, think of the writers of the Gospels as editors rather than authors. They were, of course, authors in the sense that each tells the story in his own style and from his own characteristic point of view, but they were editors inasmuch as they were working with materials which had come down to them in a traditional form. Part of this material was oral and part was written. In some cases larger collections of these sayings and stories had already been made, as in the case of the collection of the sayings of Jesus called Q.[1] No doubt it was from such independent collections of stories or sayings that the authors of Matthew and Luke drew the material which is distinctive to each of their books. The interest which the Gospels have both as literature and as records of history is greatly increased by realizing that none of them is simply

---

[1] Q stands for the German word *Quelle,* meaning *source.*

the product of a single mind selecting freely from its own recollections. Each has in a sense been written by many hands, by a multitude of unknown Christian preachers, who in special, concrete situations, drew upon the living memory of the Christian community in order to warn or console or instruct, and to proclaim anew "the wonderful works of God." So in a true and vital way, the four Gospels are the Church's books, not merely the memoirs of individual men. They are the final deposit of the mind of the primitive Church as it lived in the dawn of history's great new day and pondered the mystery of the Word made flesh.

### ST. JOHN: THE SPIRITUAL GOSPEL

THE four Gospels, as was seen at a very early period, fall naturally into two classes. The first three are so much alike in their construction and general viewpoint that they are called collectively the Synoptic Gospels.[2] When we begin to read the fourth Gospel, called by the name of ST. JOHN, we are immediately conscious of a great difference. Not only is the pattern of the book and the atmosphere which pervades it strikingly dissimilar to the Synoptic Gospels, but even the portrait of our Lord which appears upon its pages has a majesty and splendor, a depth and height, which make us feel that we never really knew Him before. In ancient times it was said that John's was the spiritual Gospel, thus distinguishing it from the other Gospels which were regarded as more *factual*. Today, it is general-

---

[2] The term *synoptic* refers to the fact that these three Gospels are so much alike that they can easily be set side by side and compared synoptically, that is with one comprehensive look.

ly agreed that the fourth Gospel is not intended to be historical in the same sense in which the Synoptics are. It is not so much an account of the life of Jesus Christ, objectively seen, as it is an appreciation of the meaning of that life. It is like a poem or drama which deals creatively with its materials in order to make evident their significance for human life and thought. It is worth noting that, whereas the Synoptic Gospels each begin with some event connected with the earthly career of our Lord, the fourth Gospel begins with the solemn words, parallel to the opening words of Genesis, *In the beginning was the Word, and the Word was with God and the Word was God.* The writer of the fourth Gospel, whoever he may have been, wants us to see the life of Jesus against the background of the whole sweep of cosmic history and to understand that in Him was incarnate the eternal truth of God. While the differences between the two types of Gospels should not be exaggerated, yet it may be stated as a rough and approximate rule that we rely more on the Synoptic Gospels for a knowledge of the external facts about the life of Christ and on the fourth Gospel for an understanding of its spiritual meaning. It is this meaning which is summarized in the second paragraph of the Nicene Creed.

### ST. MARK: THE FIRST TO BE WRITTEN

THE first of the Synoptic Gospels to be written was undoubtedly ST. MARK, the shortest, and, from a literary point of view, the least polished of them. It probably was written in Rome, shortly before 70 A.D., that is, about forty years after the crucifixion. While all the Gospels are really anonymous, yet tradition may very well be right in attributing this one to St. Mark, the friend and companion of St. Peter and St. Paul. The same tradition also says that Mark made much use of material which he remembered from the preaching of Peter. This earliest Gospel contains no stories about the birth or childhood of Jesus but begins directly with his baptism. It has probably, by accident, lost its original conclusion, since it seems to break off abruptly in the middle of a sentence *(St. Mark 16:8)* although it was later provided with another (or rather with more than one other) conclusion. The Gospel is mainly concerned with the events of the life of Jesus rather than with His teaching. Because it is the earliest record of Jesus' life extant, it is, in some ways, the most important of the Gospels.

### ST. MATTHEW: THE MOST HEBRAIC OF THE GOSPELS

THOUGH Matthew and Luke were perhaps written about the same time, ST. MATTHEW seems to represent an earlier stage than Luke in the development of Christian thought. Like Mark it was originally anonymous and the name of Matthew seems to have been attached to it because of an old tradition that this apostle made a collection of the sayings of Jesus in Aramaic and such a document has undoubtedly been used in the composition of this gospel. Both Matthew and Luke made use of the Gospel according to Mark to provide a framework for their own Gospels. They then introduced into the framework, at what seemed to them appropriate points, large fragments of the teaching of Jesus taken from a now lost collection of such teachings which scholars call simply Q. Both of them also undoubtedly made use of special oral and written traditions which were current in the localities where they worked. In Matthew the material containing our Lord's teaching has been introduced in large chunks rather than distributed more widely. The most important of these is the long section which we call the Sermon on the Mount *(chapters 5-7)*. Matthew draws upon sources peculiar to himself for the stories of the birth of Jesus, the Wise Men, the Slaughter of the Innocents by Herod, and the Flight into Egypt. The Gospel is characterized by a strongly Hebraic point of view (perhaps derived from its special source) and a constant interest in the literal fulfillment of Old Testament prophecies.

## ST. LUKE: THE MOST GENTILE OF THE GOSPELS

THE third Gospel, that according to ST. LUKE, is strikingly different from the other two since it is only the first part of a two volume history of the beginnings of Christianity. The second volume is the book called *The Acts of the Apostles.* A comparison of the opening verses of each will make it evident that these two books belong together and it is unfortunate that they are separated in the present arrangement of New Testament books. As in the case of St. Mark, it seems probable that the tradition regarding its authorship is correct, and that St. Luke, the beloved physician *(Colossians 4:14)* and the companion of Paul in many of his adventures, was the writer. Certainly it was composed by a man of taste and culture and is by far the most polished and literary of the Gospels. It was written for the benefit of a certain person called Theophilus, who is otherwise unknown.

Partly because it was intended for Gentile readers and

partly because the author was a Gentile, it has less of Hebrew spirit and flavor than the other Gospels. The author
is anxious to commend the Christian Gospel to Gentiles
and does all that he can to explain Jewish terms and customs and to make the Hebrew environment of the life
of Christ and the history of the early Church intelligible
to them.

This Gospel is marked by a gentleness of spirit which
has always been most attractive to readers of the Bible,
and many would agree with the estimate which calls it
"the most beautiful book in the world." Luke weaves the
account of our Lord's teachings more into the running
narrative than Matthew does. He also makes use of material which the other evangelists, that is writers of gospels, did not have. The nativity and childhood stories
with which he prefaces his book and which have touched
the deepest feelings of innumerable generations, the stories
of the Annunciation and Visitation, the Presentation, and
the wonderful parables of the Good Samaritan and the
Prodigal Son are all part of the rich, though unknown,
source upon which he drew.

### THE GOSPELS NOT BIOGRAPHIES, BUT GOOD NEWS

THE story which is told by all four of the writers is called
the Gospel, that is the Good News, for to the early Church
the best news possible was the announcement that the
long expected Redeemer of mankind had come. In spite
of the distinction made between the Synoptics and the
fourth Gospel, we must recognize that the differences are
largely matters of degree and that none of the Gospels is
really a biography in the modern sense of the word, since

it is not their purpose simply to convey accurate information about an interesting historical character. Each was
written with a specifically religious purpose, to show Who,
and what manner of man, the Saviour was, and to arouse
in the reader an attitude of responsive faith and love. This
purpose is explicitly set forth in the words which are the
original conclusion of the fourth Gospel, but which ap-
ply in large measure to all the Gospels, *These things are
written that ye might believe that Jesus is the Christ the
Son of God; and that believing ye might have life through
His name (St. John 20:31).* We shall not really understand these books unless we read them in this spirit, for
they are written by faith and addressed to faith, and unless the reader possesses some measure of the faith which
animates them, the real heart of their meaning will always escape him. We must read them not simply as brief
sketches of the life of one of history's great men, but as
four eloquent attempts to declare in the inadequate
language of human speech, the Good News which the
early Church had heard and which the writers had experienced: the news of the mighty work which God in
Christ had done for man.

## THE LIFE OF CHRIST
### Following chiefly the Synoptic Gospels

JUDGED by literary standards, the story which the Synoptic
writers have to tell is a simple one and is told in a direct
and simple way. The tragic elements in the plot are summarized by the fourth Gospel in the poignant words, *He
came unto His own and His own received Him not (St.
John 1:11).* The Gospel story, however, is not a tragedy

but good news and Paul states its essential content in these words, . . . *the gospel of God* . . . *concerning his Son, who was descended from David according to the flesh, and designated Son of God in power* . . . *by his resurrection from the dead (Romans 1:1-4 RSV).* The Evangelists are content to let the story make its own impression without the assistance of conscious literary art and the simplicity of their style only emphasizes the sublimity of their theme.

### JESUS' BIRTH AND CHILDHOOD

MATTHEW and Luke[3] take us back to the events connected with the birth of Jesus. St. Mary, our Lord's mother, bore Him in a stable at Bethlehem, the little town about six miles south of Jerusalem where David had been born some thousand years before. Mary and her husband, St. Joseph, had gone there in order to be enrolled in a census decreed by the Roman emperor *(St. Luke 2:1-7).* Although Jesus was born in the humblest of circumstances, yet the Evangelists tell how even then God made it clear that He was set apart from other men, for He was born of a Virgin and wonderful portents indicated that Mary's baby was no common child. Months before, the angel Gabriel had announced His birth *(St. Luke 1:26-38).* When He was born, shepherds heard choirs of angels singing above the fields outside of Bethlehem *(St. Luke 2:8-18).* Wise men of the East saw a new star shining in the sky, and Herod the king, when told that a new king was about to be born, conceived a cruel plot to

---

[3] For convenience, we shall continue in the remainder of the chapter to use the traditional names for the Gospels without implying by this any conclusions as to actual authorship.

128

destroy him *(St. Matthew 2:1-18)*. Luke includes in his story of the childhood of Jesus three beautiful hymns which have become part of the liturgy of the Church: The first, the *Magnificat,* is the song which, according to Luke's account, the Blessed Virgin sang when she knew she was to be mother of the Messiah *(St. Luke 1:46-55)*. The second, the *Benedictus,* was the song of Zacharias, the father of John the Baptist, when he learned that his son was to prepare the way of the Lord. The third, the *Nunc Dimittis,* was the song of the aged Simeon when he saw the infant Jesus in the Temple, the Child having been brought there in accordance with Jewish custom, forty days after His birth to be dedicated to God *(St. Luke 2:29-32)*.

Matthew tells how the holy family was compelled to take refuge in Egypt in order to escape the anger of Herod and how, when they returned after Herod's death, they settled in a little village called Nazareth, in the north of Palestine not far from the Lake of Galilee *(St. Matthew 2:16-23)*.

For nearly thirty years after these events, the writers of the Gospels have no stories to tell about the life of Jesus, except for a favorite reminiscence preserved in Luke which relates how Jesus, as a young boy, once visited Jerusalem with His parents and was later found in the courtyard of the Temple discussing religious questions with the learned teachers of Israel. These were the hidden years in the life of Jesus, in which His mind and character were developing and He was growing in the consciousness of who He was and what His destiny was to be. We should like to know more about this period, but that merely indicates how different our point of view is from that of the Evangelists.[4] As we have seen above, they were not writing biographies in the modern style and so were not interested in what we should call the psychological development of their hero. They had but one concern, to confront the reader with a personal challenge to faith, the challenge which is implicit in the story of our Lord's public life. The story they tell is not one which can be read merely with interest and detachment. It is a gospel, as Mark says, *the gospel of Jesus Christ the Son of God (St. Mark 1:1)* and the reader must either accept or reject the Good News which it brings and the claim to personal devotion which it makes. Since it is the Evangelists' purpose either to bring the reader to this choice or to strengthen him in a choice which has already been made, they get as quickly as possible to the heart of their story. The Gospel of St. Mark actually begins at this point—with our Lord's baptism. Even in the other Gospels, what precedes is merely by way of preface.

### JESUS BEGINS HIS PUBLIC MINISTRY IN GALILEE

THE public ministry of Jesus began when he was about the age of thirty and in all the Gospels is brought into connection with the work of John the Baptist. John, who, according to Luke, was a close relative of Jesus, was an eloquent preacher of righteousness who both lived and spoke in the manner of the Old Testament prophets. He

---

[4] Christians of the post-apostolic age had the same kind of curiosity we have and produced innumerable fanciful stories about the birth and childhood of Jesus. These are recorded in the so-called Apocryphal Gospels, which though historically unreliable, are valuable as the product of a certain naïve and touching kind of early Christian piety.

exerted a powerful influence upon the people of his day, as recorded also by the contemporary Jewish historian Josephus. Great crowds followed him and underwent the symbolic ceremony of bathing in the Jordan river. By this they indicated their desire to cleanse themselves of sin in preparation for the coming of God's kingdom, an event which John prophesied for the immediate future and painted in bold and terrifying colors. Among those who heard him and who received the baptism of repentance was Jesus and it was this event which seems to have crystallized the thoughts regarding God's purpose for His life which had been taking shape in His mind. As he emerged from the waters, He heard the voice of God speaking to Him and declaring, *Thou art my beloved son in whom I am well pleased (St. Mark 1:11)*. He now knew Himself to be the Messiah, the Son of God.

Jesus felt Himself called first of all to the same kind of public preaching ministry which John had exercised, but before he began it wished to have a time of quiet preparation. For this purpose he went alone into the rough, desert region which lay between Jerusalem and the Dead Sea and in that solitude struggled with a series of temptations *(St. Matthew 4:1-10)*. There was the temptation to misuse his newly discovered powers of messiahship for selfish ends (making stones become bread), or merely to play the role of the familiar oriental wonder-worker (casting Himself down from the temple), or to achieve His purpose by unworthy means (worshipping the devil). By the grace of God he rejected them all and *angels came and ministered unto him (St. Matthew 4:11)*. It was only after He had thus faced the stern realities of the life to which

He was called that He began to preach, as John had done before Him, *The Kingdom of God is at hand; repent and believe this good news (St. Mark 1:15).*

John had preached in Judea in the neighborhood of Jerusalem, but Jesus carried on His ministry in the north where His own home was. Although He preached once in Nazareth, He learned that *No prophet is acceptable in his own country (St. Luke 4:24),* and afterwards confined His activity largely to the fishing villages along the shore of the nearby Lake of Galilee. This early time of public teaching is called The Galilean Ministry.

### THE TEACHING OF JESUS

DURING this period, our Lord's activities fall naturally into three main parts: His public teaching, His miracles, and His private teaching to His disciples. His public preaching was concerned with proclaiming the imminent approach of the Kingdom of God and with showing what it was like, and what great changes its coming, and even its near approach, must bring. His method of teaching was almost never that of learned argument, but rather the telling of stories (parables as they are called), in each one of which He intended to make clear some point, and only one point, about God and His Kingdom and the new situation created by the coming of that Kingdom. In reading the parables today it is necessary to remember this purpose. They are not designed to state universal moral principles or to give general suggestions for happy and successful living. They are primarily intended to show men what God is like, what the laws of His Kingdom are, and what the coming of the Kingdom will mean.

132

Certain of the parables set forth, in story form, the true character of God. The parable of *The Prodigal Son,* for example, *(St. Luke 15:11-32)* pictures God's inexhaustible love, a love which is always awaiting the return of the prodigal, and is "always more ready to hear than we to pray." The parable of *The Sower and the Seed (St. Mark 4:1-9; St. Matthew 13:1-9; St. Luke 8:4-8)* describes the inevitable triumph of God's plans. God's Word is of such power, that, despite all the hindrances which human nature can interpose, it will eventually find a lodging place in good ground and bring forth an hundredfold.

Other parables show what kind of people will be likely to accept the message of the Kingdom and become its citizens. They reflect our Lord's actual experience in finding a more receptive audience among the poor and outcast than among the religiously and socially respectable scribes and Pharisees. The most familiar of the parables of this type is that of *The Pharisee and the Publican (St. Luke 18:9-14).* The man who was acceptable in God's sight was not the self-satisfied, though morally irreproachable Pharisee. The better man, in God's eyes, was the tax collector whose greedy and dishonest life was quite properly despised by his fellow countrymen, but who realized his own failure and was "of a humble and contrite spirit." The message of the parable of *The Two Sons (St. Matthew 21:28-32)* and of *The Rich Man and Lazarus (St. Luke 16:19-31)* is similar. In the parable of *The Wicked Husbandmen (St. Mark 12:1-12; St. Matthew 21:33-45; St. Luke 20:9-18),* Jesus predicts His own death at the hands of those who should have been the first to receive Him. In the parable of *The Marriage Feast (St. Matthew*

*22:1-10; St. Luke 14:15-24)* he declares that the place in the Kingdom which was first offered to the conventionally religious people of that day will be taken by those whom they regard as the scum of the streets. The repellent figure of the elder brother in *The Prodigal Son* is also modelled after that of the smug and haughty Pharisee; while the prodigal is a portrait of "the publicans and sinners."

Still other parables describe the character of the true citizen of the Kingdom and the laws by which he lives. The parable of *The Good Samaritan (St. Luke 10:29-37)* pictures the all-inclusive love which must prevail where God is King and national and racial boundaries are necessarily broken down. God's demand for a forgiving spirit is set forth in the parable of *The Unmerciful Servant (St. Matthew 18:23-35)*. Men may not pray "forgive us our trespasses" unless they can also say "as we forgive those who trespass against us."

Another group of parables sets forth specifically the imminence of judgment and the coming of the Kingdom and warns men to be ready when it comes. The most familiar of these is the parable of *The Wise and Foolish Virgins (St. Matthew 25:1-13)*. Similar in general thought are the parables of *The House Built Upon the Rock (St. Matthew 7:24-27; St. Luke 6:48-49)* and that of *The Rich Fool (St. Luke 12:13-21)*. Both the parable of *The Talents (St. Matthew 25:14-30; St. Luke 19:11-27)* and that of *The Unjust Steward (St. Luke 16:1-12)* teach that "the sons of light" should show as much imaginative zeal in the affairs of God and His Kingdom and in using the privileges which it brings, as clever citizens of the world show in furthering their own selfish and even immoral ends. The parable of *The Tares (St. Matthew 13:24-30; 36-43)* warns those whose impatience would lead them to pass hasty judgment upon others that vengeance belongs only to God and that in His own good time He will exercise it. The parable of *The Laborers in the Vineyard (St. Matthew 20:1-16)* is perplexing to many, but its point is really the Pauline doctrine of "justification by faith." Whatever God gives to us either by way of special favors now, or reward in the day of reckoning, is given out of the richness of His grace and is not bestowed upon us as a salary paid for services rendered.

Almost all the parables had some direct concern with the astonishing fact that the Kingdom of God was then at hand and perhaps, in some sense, was already there. A new age of the world had begun and the powers of the coming Kingdom were already at work. *Old things are passed away; behold all things are become new (II Corinthians 5:17).* One cannot understand the New Testament unless he first realizes this sense of living in a new period of world history which permeates it. And one cannot share the Christian faith today unless he also has the feeling that the Kingdom of God is near to us also and that we are still standing in its dawning light.

With this new age a change necessarily had to take place in the kind of religious and ethical system under which men were living. So in the Sermon on the Mount *(St. Matthew 5-7),* we hear the reiterated refrain, *Ye have heard that it was said by them of old time . . . ; but I say unto you.* Men were no longer to live as before under the rigid rule of codified law and statute, but rather to live by the law of God which is written in their hearts. This did not mean a relaxation of the stringency of God's demands, but rather a tightening of them. Once, murder had been forbidden; now, it was also forbidden to hate one's enemy in his heart. Once, sexual impurity was forbidden; now, one must not even tolerate impure thoughts. Under the New Covenant, hate is murder; lust is adultery. Once, men had been permitted to retaliate in kind for injuries done them; now, they were under obligation to forgive those who ill-used them and go to almost any extreme to avoid anger and the spirit of revenge. Once, there had been a multiplicity of particular statutes to govern life; now, there was but one law which was to be applied to every conceivable situation in life, the law of love toward God and Man *(St. Mark 12:29-31). A new commandment I give unto you, that ye love one another (St. John 13:34).* These things were the laws of the Kingdom of God and, since men stood upon the threshold of the Kingdom, they must strive, as far as humanly possible, to act according to them. They must already begin to live as citizens of God's Kingdom. Although the rule[5] of God is called a kingdom yet the King Himself is called our Father which means that in His realm, men must live with Him as children and with each other as brothers.

## JESUS' MINISTRY OF HEALING

OUR Lord's work was by no means confined only to teaching. We have already noticed how indifferent St. Mark's Gospel seems to this side of His activity. To the people of Jesus' day, certainly, the strongest evidence of the truth

---

[5] The word translated *kingdom* in the New Testament corresponds closely to our English word *reign* or *rule*. It has none of the geographical implications we attach, for example, to the phrase Kingdom of England.

of His claim to be the inaugurator of a new age was to be seen in His ability to heal the sick. There one could plainly see "the powers of the age to come." He Himself said, *If I with the finger of God cast out demons, no doubt the kingdom of God is come upon you (St. Luke 11:20).* Consequently, much of the Gospel story is taken up with the stories of His power to cast out demons (for insanity and many other afflictions were in these days believed to be the work of evil spirits), to heal all kinds of diseases, and even to raise the dead. It may well be that some of these stories have been heightened in the telling and that tradition has conveyed them to us in a form which, to some extent, reflects the convictions of the early Christians. On the other hand, the stories of healing are too many and too basic merely to be explained away. There are too many to be discussed even briefly here and they all give striking testimony to the fact that wherever Jesus went He left the impression that He was One who had the power to do such things. Men felt that He was surrounded by an aura of healing strength which was the best evidence that God was with Him. Because of the things He could do men could believe the things which He said.

## THE CHOICE OF THE TWELVE

ALMOST from the beginning Jesus began to attract followers and among these He chose twelve, the number of the tribes of Israel, to be His special emissaries. Their names were Peter, James and John, Andrew, Philip, Bartholomew, Matthew, Thomas, James the Less, Jude or Thaddaeus, Simon the Zealot, and Judas Iscariot *(St. Mark 3:13-19).* These simple, otherwise quite obscure, men were called apostles, that is men sent, representatives bearing a special commission. The twelve travelled about with Jesus and formed the nucleus of a new spiritual fellowship. This was the beginning of the Church in one sense of the word, although in another and profounder sense, the Church was not new at all. It was merely the faithful heart of the old Israel, the remnant of which Isaiah had spoken, out of which the new and greater Israel of the Christian Church was to grow. With this inner group of disciples, Jesus had a special kind of life. They shared their meals together in a religious fellowship, held their money in common, and, like other religious fellowships within Israel, celebrated the Sabbath and other great days of the Jewish calendar by taking part in a sacred meal. The Last Supper was, literally, the last of these fellowship meals. Beside this stable inner group of specially trained and disciplined apostles, there was also a larger and more indefinite group of disciples (that is pupils), whose numbers varied considerably from time to time. This is illustrated by one occasion on which Jesus was able to send out seventy of them as heralds of the Gospel *(St. Luke 10:1)*. Probably the time of our Lord's greatest popularity is marked by the story of the Feeding of the Five Thousand *(St. Mark 6:31-44)*.

### ENEMIES BEGIN TO OPPOSE JESUS' WORK

ONE whose ministry was attended with such outstanding initial success, and whose teaching was by its nature opposed in so many points to that of the religious leaders of the time, was bound to make enemies. The scribes, who were the official religious teachers of the people, and the

Pharisees, who were the dominant sect in Judaism at that day, attacked His work almost from the beginning *(St. Mark 2:1, 3, 6, 7)*. They were opposed to the freedom with which He ventured to interpret the Jewish Law, even though He was careful to observe its major provisions, and were offended by His tolerant attitude toward the less respectable classes of the community, "the lesser breeds without the Law." He also aroused the enmity of Herod Antipas, tetrarch of Galilee, a son of the Herod who had been king when Jesus was born. Herod had already executed John the Baptist for criticizing his illegal marriage to his brother's wife *(St. Mark 6:14-29)* and he was not likely to treat Jesus more gently if sufficient occasion presented itself. Faced by this rising tide of opposition, Jesus seems for a while to have turned from a public to a more private kind of ministry and we find Him even going with His followers beyond the borders of Israel into Syria to the north *(the coasts of Tyre and Sidon, St. Mark 7:24)*.

### PETER DECLARES JESUS TO BE THE CHRIST

ACCORDING to the Synoptic Gospels, our Lord had little to say with regard to His own person in the early part of His ministry, although He always spoke and acted with an authority which implied that He was no mere human teacher. *They were astonished at his doctrine; for he taught them as one that had authority and not as the scribes (St. Mark 1:22)*. He felt that His main task was to preach about the coming of the Kingdom and to manifest in His healing miracles the powers of the new age. The nature of His preaching and the mighty works which He did were sufficient evidence of who He was. *Go and show*

*John again those things which ye do see and hear (St. Matthew 11:2-6).*

At last, however, the time seemed ripe to test the convictions of His followers, and, at Caesarea Philippi, Peter freely declared his faith that Jesus was the Messiah whom the Jews had been looking for for so many centuries. *Thou art the Christ of God (St. Mark 8:29; St. Luke 9:20).* It was important that the disciples should have come to this conclusion independently, for now that they understood the place He occupied in the plan of God, Jesus could go on another step and explain what kind of Messiah He was to be. For He knew that His messiahship was not to be patterned as most people expected, on the lines of a military leader, like David. He found the plan of His life in a part of the Old Testament which was not ordinarily interpreted as referring to the Messiah, the mysterious fifty-third chapter of Isaiah, which told of one who was to suffer and die for the sins of His people and at last to be raised up a victor. Because of this our Lord knew His ministry must end in tragedy and He told His followers that suffering and death were to be His lot *(St. Mark 8:31).* The disciples, who were still thinking in quite different terms, seem not to have understood what He meant until these things actually came to pass. Shortly after this crucial scene at Caesarea Philippi, three of the apostles were with him on a mountain top and there saw Him transfigured, surrounded by heavenly glory. At that moment, although they failed to grasp its full significance, they had a brief foretaste of our Lord's triumph over sin and death and His eternal reign as King *(St. Mark 9:2-8).* There were many such things of which they saw the true meaning only in after years.[6]

## JESUS GOES UP TO JERUSALEM

THESE events brought Jesus' Galilean ministry to a close. Now recognized for what He knew Himself to be and the foundation of the new, spiritual Israel firmly laid in the fellowship of His apostles, it remained only for the pattern which God had prescribed for His life to be realized. Speedily He turned His face toward Jerusalem where He knew that He must die *(St. Mark 10:1)*. To many people of the modern world this deliberate choice of a road which could end only in death seems almost perverse. Why should He not have stayed in Galilee and continued to do good, healing the sick, and teaching His way of life? The answer is that He did not believe that this was what God wanted Him to do. As God's Messiah, it was His appointed destiny *to give his life a ransom for many (St. Mark 10:45)*. Even regarded from the practical standpoint of human history, His name would hardly be known to us today if He had continued to be only a Galilean prophet and teacher. Because He went up to Jerusalem and there *for the joy that was set before him, endured the cross, despising the shame (Hebrews 12:2)*, the ages have called Him Lord.

It was the custom among the Jews to celebrate, when possible, the great feast of the Passover in Jerusalem, and

---

[6] Some scholars believe that the Synoptic Gospels tend to oversimplify the account of our Lord's self-consciousness and the growing realization of the significance of His life on the part of the apostles. The fourth Gospel, it should be noted, presents a somewhat different picture. Nevertheless we can be sure that the narrative in the Synoptic Gospels does not distort the essential truth.

large groups of pilgrims went up each year. It was with such a group as this that Jesus and the Twelve went up from Galilee to begin the last dramatic scene of His brief career. He may have made other journeys to Jerusalem in previous years, as the fourth Gospel suggests, but if He did, the Synoptic Gospels make no mention of the fact. For them it was the last journey which was significant for faith and it was only at the end of this last journey that His brief Judean ministry can be said to have begun.

All the Evangelists have some incidents to record which took place on the road to Jerusalem, Luke more than the others *(St. Luke 9:51–19:28)*. The route which Jesus and the disciples took led them through Perea (modern Transjordan) to the city of Jericho near the head of the Dead Sea. From Jericho the pilgrims had to climb the steep road from the Jordan Valley to Jerusalem. As they approached the Holy City by the road which led over the Mount of Olives and down into the Kedron ravine, the disciples of Jesus, at His command, fulfilled the ancient prophecy in Zechariah 9:9. *Shout, O daughter of Jerusalem; behold thy King cometh unto thee . . . lowly and riding upon an ass and upon a colt the foal of an ass (St. Mark 11:1-10)*. In lowly dignity, enthroned as Prince of Peace, Jesus rode into the Holy City. He could not have chosen a clearer way to declare that He was the promised deliverer of Israel.

## "DESPISED AND REJECTED OF MEN"

WITH the triumphal entry on the first day of the week, the tragic concluding act in the drama of Jesus' life began to unfold. Each night He and His disciples went out of the city and stayed with friends in the little town of Bethany, but each day He came into Jerusalem and continued His ministry of teaching.

On Monday He went into the Temple and His anger was aroused when He saw it desecrated by the buying and selling of animals for sacrifice and by the changing of money within the sacred precincts. With the authority which was His as God's Messiah, He drove out the merchants single-handed and purified the Temple courts. It was this which led directly to His death, since the leaders of the people realized that His claims to power were now so sweeping that He could not be dismissed as a harmless fanatic. His claim to authority and the manner in which He used it was a direct challenge to their own *(St. Mark 11:15-18)*. In Jerusalem, He came not merely in conflict with the scribes and Pharisees, as in Galilee, but with the Sadducees, the priestly, aristocratic party who actually governed the nation and were no doubt chiefly responsible for bringing about His death. His enemies began to consult together as to the best manner of removing Him from the scene in correct legal fashion and without creating too much disturbance. Their plot was considerably furthered when one of His disciples, Judas Iscariot, offered to help them carry out their plans, perhaps because he was disappointed at Jesus' failure to act with the vigor he thought necessary for one who claimed the throne of David *(St. Mark 14:10, 11)*.

At last the time for celebrating the Passover Feast drew near. The fourth Gospel is probably correct in representing the Last Supper which Jesus had with His disciples, not as the actual Passover Meal, but as a preparatory meal held the night before *(St. John 13:1; 19:14)*. This, at least, is the tradition which the Church follows in its observance of Holy Week. On Thursday night Jesus and the Twelve engaged an upper room and celebrated a fellowship meal which was part of the solemn ceremonies connected with the Passover. There, as related in the fourth Gospel *(St. John 13:1-12)*, Jesus washed the feet of the disciples, giving a practical demonstration of the meaning of the spirit of brotherhood and mutual helpfulness which was to mark the common life of Christians. During the meal He took some of the bread and before He distributed it to the disciples, said, *Take eat, this is my body.* After this He took the cup of wine and, when He had given thanks, said, *This is my blood of the covenant* and gave it to the disciples to drink. He commanded that this action should always be repeated among them in grateful remembrance of the sacrificial death which He was about to die *(St. Mark 14:22-24; I Corinthians 11:23-29)*. The Church has always understood that His words, *This is my body* and *This is my blood,* involved a promise that whenever His followers repeated this sacred rite, which they came to call the Lord's Supper, Jesus Himself would in some mysterious way really be present in their midst. The eating of the bread would be a communion of the Body of Christ, and the drinking of the wine a communion of His blood *(I Corinthians 10:16)*.

After supper was over, they all went outside the city to a secluded garden called Gethsemane, on the side of the Mount of Olives, and there Jesus spent the remainder of the time in prayer and in a struggle with His own natural reluctance to face the ordeal which confronted

144

Him (*St. Mark 14:32-36; St. Luke 22:39-44*). It was to the garden that Judas, who knew His plans, brought the Jewish temple police to apprehend Him.

From the garden He was taken to the palace of Caiaphas, the high priest, where He was hastily examined before a court composed of the high priest and his associates. In answer to the high priest's question, He publicly claimed the title of Messiah which Peter had been the first to give Him. In view of the defiant attitude He had previously taken toward many of the customs, and particularly the authorities of the nation, this was sufficient to secure the unanimous verdict that He must die (*St. Mark 14:53-65*). Since Jewish courts were forbidden by their Roman overlords to carry out a capital sentence, He was remanded to the court of Pilate and the same morning (Friday) brought before the Roman governor to have His case reviewed. Because the charge of blasphemy under which He had previously been convicted was a purely religious one and could not possibly carry weight with the secular power, He was now accused of rebellion against the authority of the emperor in that He set Himself up to be The King of the Jews. Pilate saw through the stratagem and made a feeble effort to defend Jesus, but, being already in bad grace with both the Jews and his Roman superiors because of previous acts of arrogance and greed, he felt it politic in the long run to conciliate his subjects and acquiesce in the decision of the Jewish authorities (*St. Mark 15:1-15*). Pilate's naïve attempt to shift responsibility for the decision in no way alters the fact that it was Pilate who passed the sentence of death and his soldiers who executed it.

So at last Jesus was condemned to die by the cruel method of crucifixion, the method used by the Romans for the execution of slaves and criminals of the lowest class. A short distance outside the city, at a place called Golgotha, somewhere about noon on Friday, He and two thieves were hung upon crosses together. There, through long hours of agony, He accomplished the destiny he knew God intended for Him. There *He was numbered with the transgressors and bare the sin of many (Isaiah 53:12).* As He hung upon the cross, He spoke several times, and each of the Gospels records certain of the words He said, seven sentences in all *(St. Mark 15:34; St. Luke 23:34, 43, 46; St. John 19:26, 27, 28, 30).* These last words which He spoke have taken their place among the Church's most precious devotional treasures. Before the agony (the Passion) began, He had refused the drink which was offered to Him to dull His mind and relieve the pain, so He was fully conscious as He approached the end and finally committed His spirit to God. The Roman officer who supervised the execution and had watched the progress of His suffering, looked upon His crucified body and said in admiration, *Truly this man was a son of God (St. Mark 15:39 RSV).* Because of the Passover festival, Jesus was buried as quickly as possible. So far as His enemies were concerned, the case was closed and the authorities, both secular and spiritual, no doubt slept more quietly that night in the knowledge that another potential troublemaker was safely out of the way. Even for the disciples, His death marked the end of everything. They had not realized that He was going to die and therefore they had no expectation of a resurrection. They had never really understood that Jesus' messiahship was not to be patterned after the life of a warrior-king like David, but rather after the model of the mysterious Suffering Servant described by the unknown prophet of the Exile. He was not to rule in the midst of His enemies *(Psalm 110:2)*, but to be *despised and rejected of men (Isaiah 53:3).*

## "THE THIRD DAY HE ROSE AGAIN"

THROUGHOUT His whole ministry Jesus had insistently proclaimed His belief in the Kingdom of God. The burden of His preaching had been that it is God who rules the world and the day when that rule will be completely actualized among men is near at hand. It was in that faith that He died and it was by the power of that faith that He rose from the dead. On Sunday morning three women came to the tomb to perform the last services which the living can offer to the dead and to their amazement discovered that the tomb was empty and the Lord was gone *(St. Mark 16:1-8).* In the days that followed He appeared in unmistakable form to many of His disciples in different times and places: to Mary Magdalene and the women *(St. Matthew 28:9, 10),* to Peter *(St. Luke 24:34; I Corinthians 15:5),* to the eleven remaining apostles *(St. Matthew 28:16, 17; St. Luke 24:36-48; St. John 20:19-23),* and to two disciples as they were walking toward Emmaus, a little village near Jerusalem *(St. Luke 24:13-35).* The earliest account of the resurrection appearances, that in I Corinthians 15:5-8, mentions also appearances to more than five hundred disciples on some otherwise unspecified occasion and to James, a member of Jesus' own family, who had not previously been among His followers. This does not exhaust the list of appearances but is enough to suggest their variety and the tense excitement of those days.

The very existence of the New Testament and the Christian Church is the surest proof that these stories are not the product of illusion but evidence of the most stupendous event in the history of man, an event which marked the end of one great age of world history and the beginning of a new. Nothing in the previous story of the disciples is adequate to explain the things which now began to happen. They were simple, ignorant, even cowardly men, as their behavior at the time of their Lord's deepest extremity showed all too clearly. Yet, as a result of these awe-inspiring experiences which, contrary to all their expectation, convinced them that Jesus was indeed the Son of God *(Romans 1:4)*, they began to preach the Gospel with such conviction that the Church spread within a few decades throughout the Mediterranean world.

Christ Himself had always known what the result of His death would be, for He knew that the eternal purpose of God cannot be defeated. His death was only the beginning. It was not to be the end of His work but to be the means by which the power of God would overcome the power of sin and death and inaugurate the new and last age of the world, the age of the Church and of the Holy Spirit of God. In that age, however long it might endure in terms of human time, men would always be standing at the threshold of God's Kingdom. The powers of that Kingdom would be available to all who chose to claim them and to shape their lives according to its laws.

## "AND SITTETH ON THE RIGHT HAND OF GOD"

THE story of the Ascension marks the end of the earthly
ministry of Jesus. From this time forward He was The
Lord, the glorious King who had taken up His rule over
all creation, to whom the Church applied not only the
language which the Old Testament uses for the Messiah, but even the language which is there used only of
God. There could be no doubt in the mind of Jesus' followers that this Man who had lived so simply and trag-
ically upon earth was no mere prophet, nor even merely
the long-promised Messiah. No categories derived from
human experience were adequate to describe Him. He
could be no other than a manifestation of the Eternal God
Himself. The fourth Gospel, which endeavors to set forth
in dramatic form the spiritual significance of His life, reveals Him as such from the first page to the last. It begins
with the statement that the Word by which God created
the universe and which Itself was God *was made flesh and
dwelt among us (St. John 1:1-14)*. It ends with the confession of Thomas who fell before the Risen Jesus and cried
*My Lord and my God (St. John 20:28)*. The fourth Gospel
was written in order to show that for those who had eyes
to see and faith to understand the whole earthly career of
Jesus could be seen, in retrospect, as suffused with the
Glory of God, and that from first to last it was the
story of One who was *God of God, Light of Light, Very
God of Very God.*

CHAPTER
NINE

# The Acts: *How the Church Spread from Jerusalem to Rome*

THE new age which began with the Resurrection of Jesus was and is the Age of the Church. Therefore, the rest of the New Testament is the first chapter in Church history. It tells how that little group of men whom our Lord had chosen during His Galilean ministry became the center of an expanding Church and how that Church gradually overflowed the banks of the old national Israel and began to spread its power and healing influence among the Gentiles. The prophecy of the Second Isaiah was fulfilled, *The Gentiles shall come to thy light and kings to the brightness of thy rising.* So slowly out of the Old Israel the Holy Catholic Church was born.

## PETER AND THE CHURCH AT JERUSALEM

LUKE's second volume, THE ACTS OF THE APOSTLES, which begins with an account of the Ascension, has this story for its theme. It opens in Jerusalem; it ends in Rome. The

history of the Church, which seemed to have begun merely as an obscure Jewish sect in Jerusalem, is traced until
in the last chapter it is found firmly established in Rome,
the great capital of the Gentile world. The first fifteen
chapters are largely concerned with the Jerusalem Church
and St. Peter is the principal figure. These chapters tell
how after the Ascension, the apostles chose Matthias to
take the place of Judas the traitor and how, on the day
of Pentecost, they received God's Holy Spirit and immediately began to manifest those wonderful powers which
were so marked a feature of the early days of the Church
(*Acts 1, 2*). It also records the manner of life of that early
Church in Jerusalem and how it attempted to realize to
the full the spirit of Christian brotherhood. Many, perhaps most, of the members sold their private possessions
and agreed to hold all their property in common. Luke
says no one called any of the things which he possessed his
own (*Acts 4:32-35*).

Already in this early Church there were men called
Hellenists, who though Jews, had a Greek background
and were more sympathetic to the emancipating influences
of the Gospel than those disciples whose background was
purely Jewish and Palestinian. The leaders of this group
were the seven men whom the apostles appointed to ad-
minister the community's common funds and who thereby became the first members of the order of deacons (*Acts
6:1-6*). Because of their liberal ideas these men, far more
than any of the original twelve, aroused the enmity of the
Jewish leaders, and St. Stephen, the chief of them, was
stoned to death (*Acts 6:8–8:2*). The persecution of this
group forced them to flee from Jerusalem, and from their

flight arose incidentally the first missionary work amongst non-Jews: the conversion of some Samaritans and of the Ethiopian Eunuch; the spread of the Gospel to Antioch *(Acts 8; 11:19, 20).*

This mission to the Gentiles is the theme with which the book of Acts now becomes chiefly concerned. Paul, who up to this time had been a violent enemy of the Church and had set out on a journey from Jerusalem to Damascus to persecute the Christians there, was overwhelmed on the way by a vision of the Risen Jesus and himself accepted the faith. This was a crucial event in the life of the Church, for Paul was to become the greatest thinker of the apostolic age as well as the great apostle to the Gentiles *(Acts 9).* Peter also became convinced of the value of the Gentile mission and succeeded in getting the Church at Jerusalem to endorse it *(Acts 10, 11).*

### THE BEGINNINGS OF GENTILE CHRISTIANITY

THE center of the story now shifts almost imperceptibly from Jerusalem, the home of Jewish Christianity, to Antioch, which soon became the mother city of Gentile Christianity. It was there that the followers of Jesus first came to be distinguished from the Jews of the Old Israel by the name of Christians *(Acts 11:26).* It was from Antioch, more than a decade after Paul's conversion, that Paul and Barnabas, accompanied at the beginning by Mark, set out upon the first of the great missionary journeys which were to carry the name of Christ through every province between Jerusalem and the capital of the Empire *(Acts 13, 14).* This time the two of them did not go far, but contented themselves with preaching in the island of Cyprus, and, after crossing over to the mainland of Asia Minor, in the inland cities of Pisidian Antioch, Iconium, Lystra, and Derbe. They met with many adventures, as on all the missionary journeys, and were constantly opposed by the Jews, who were now becoming aware that they were faced by a genuine revolutionary movement and not merely by the rise of a new sect within Judaism.

Wherever Paul went, he found Jewish communities, the Dispersion, and he almost always began his work in any new city by preaching in the local synagogue, where a new and learned rabbi from abroad always was welcome. It was only natural that he should do so, for the earliest Christians thought of themselves as still belonging to the synagogue and regarded the Gospel as the logical consummation of all for which Judaism stood. Paul made a few converts this way, but on the whole the results were discouraging and time and again he found himself compelled to turn to the Gentiles (e.g. Acts 13:42-48). Because of the low state to which religion had fallen in the pagan Greco-Roman world, he found among the Gentiles much more fertile soil for the Word of God. The first communities which Paul visited on the Asiatic mainland were in the Roman Province of Galatia and it is probably to them that his epistle to the Galatians was later directed.

On their return to Syrian Antioch, the missionaries found that a crisis had arisen in the Church over the terms on which the Gentiles might be admitted to the Christian fellowship. There was an older group of Jewish Christians, belonging to the community in Jerusalem, which felt that the ceremonial and dietary laws which God had laid on the Old Israel were still in force in the New. This group insisted that Gentiles who became Christians must of necessity first become Jews by accepting the initiatory rite of circumcision and by keeping strictly all the complex ritual requirements of the Law of Moses. They were demanding that the Church at Antioch accept their views.

Paul, who had fallen under the influence of St. Stephen and the Hellenists, and was a powerful and original thinker in his own right, was convinced that the Old Law had been completely done away in Christ. He and Barnabas were sent up to Jerusalem to present to a council consisting of the apostles and presbyters of the mother Church a reasoned exposition of Paul's liberal interpretation of the Gospel. They were to defend the practice which had come to prevail in the Church at Antioch and in the churches founded by Paul according to which Gentiles were admitted to full membership in the Church on the ground of baptism and profession of faith in Christ alone, without being required to observe the Jewish law. In form the decision finally arrived at by the council *(Acts 15)* seemed like a compromise. The new Gentile converts were ordered henceforth to avoid certain practices which might give serious offense to their Jewish brethren. Actually, though, the decision was a complete vindication of the teaching of Paul and the practice of the Hellenistic churches and from this time on there could be no serious question that Paul's gospel had triumphed and that the future of Christianity lay with the Gentiles. Had the old restrictions prevailed in the Church contrary to the spirit of Christ, an insuperable barrier would have been set up to the progress of the Christian message among non-Jews; now that those restrictions had been removed by authority of the Jerusalem council, the way was opened for that tremendous influx of a spiritually hungry Gentile world which was to characterize the immediately following centuries. In the artistic structure of the Book of Acts, the decision marks the beginning of a new epoch. In this one dramatic scene the author would have us see how Israel burst the boundaries of nationality and became a Universal, or Catholic, Church.

### PAUL AND THE CHURCH OF THE GENTILES

QUITE naturally, the second half of the Book of Acts, which begins at chapter 16, is entirely devoted to the work of Paul, and to the further rapid spread of the Church among the Gentiles. Since Paul and Barnabas were unable to agree on giving another chance to Mark, who had deserted them on the first journey, they decided to go different ways, and Paul took Silas with him as companion on his second missionary journey. They briefly revisited the churches of South Galatia which had been founded on the first journey, were joined by Timothy, a young convert from Derbe, and quickly then pressed on across Asia. At Troas, on the shores of the Hellespont, Paul received a vision which convinced him that God wished him to carry the Gospel into Europe *(Acts 16:1-9)*. He then crossed over to Greece and in short order preached and founded churches at Philippi, Thessalonica, and Berea. During much of this time, Luke, the author of the book, was his companion. At Athens, where Paul hoped to make a great impression by presenting his Gospel persuasively in such terms as would appeal to Greek philosophical thought, he suffered his one great failure *(Acts 17:16-34)* and resolved from that time on to proclaim the Good News simply and unaffectedly for what it was *(I Corinthians 1:22-24; 2:1-5)*. Strong in this resolution, he visited Corinth, where he stayed for eighteen months and, after meeting with another sharp rebuff from the Jews, devoted himself to preaching with enormous success to Gentiles alone *(Acts 18:1-17)*. After having preached briefly at Ephesus, he at last returned to Jerusalem and Antioch *(Acts 18:18-22)*.

His third missionary journey began at Antioch, as did all the others, and took him straight across country to Ephesus *(Acts 18:23, 24; 19:1)*, where for more than two years he preached and taught daily in a local lecture hall, after another unsuccessful attempt to work through the synagogue *(Acts 19:8-14)*. Here he had an exciting and typical adventure with the partisans of Artemis, the patron goddess of the city *(Acts 19:23-41)*. Having made a brief visit to the churches he had established in Greece and in northern Asia Minor, he returned to Palestine and, in spite of prophetic warnings that serious danger lay ahead, completed his third journey by returning to Jerusalem. Quite innocently, while visiting the temple, he became involved in a riot and was saved from violent death only by the interposition of the Roman authorities, who placed him in protective custody *(Acts 20, 21)*.

The remainder of the book *(Acts 21:33–28:31)* tells the story of his adventures as a prisoner of the Romans. He was kept under guard at Caesarea, the Roman seat of administration in Palestine, for more than two years and received hearings under two successive governors, Felix and Festus, and at last before Agrippa II, a minor king of the

Herodian line whom Festus asked to guide him in the disposition of the case. After Paul's eloquent defense of himself before the king, Agrippa advised that he could have been freed if he had not already taken advantage of his Roman citizenship and made a formal appeal to the emperor. Since he had done so, the case could be settled only in the imperial court and Paul was sent on the long, dangerous voyage to Rome.

The chapter (27) which tells of the sea trip is one of the most remarkable travel narratives which have come down to us from ancient times and is full of the excitement which only an eye-witness, such as Luke, could communicate. At last, after a shipwreck on the island of Malta and many other adventures, Paul arrived safely at Rome where he spent two years in mild imprisonment. This permitted him a good deal of liberty, and he was able to continue his preaching of the Gospel. Here in Rome he wrote the Epistles to the Philippians, Colossians, Philemon, and, possibly, Ephesians.

At this point, the Book of Acts comes to an end without any hint as to how Paul's trial came out. Some believe that he was condemned and executed shortly afterward. According to tradition, he was acquitted and continued his missionary work for a few years, only to be rearrested and executed with St. Peter at the time of the first persecution of the Christians under Nero in 64 A.D. Luke, however, tells nothing of this. His story ends when he has given a dramatic illustration of the way in which the center of gravity in the Church passed from the Jews to the Gentiles, from Jerusalem to Rome. The hero of Luke's book is neither Peter nor Paul, but the Holy Spirit which was quietly working to bring all things into accord with God's eternal plan. When Acts ends, the Church is already established and carrying on her work in the form which God intended her to have, and the developments which followed belong rather to Church history than to the creative and normative age which is pictured in the New Testament.

# The Epistles: *Life in the*
# *New Testament Church*

THE rest of the New Testament consists
mostly of letters written to churches or to church offi-
cials of the apostolic age. These letters are not general
treatises on Christian doctrine, but (for the most part) are
directed to some concrete situation in the life of a particular Christian congregation. In order to understand any
one of them, it is necessary to know something about the
life and situation of the church to which it is addressed.
In order to understand them as a whole, one must have in
mind a general picture of life in the apostolic Church.

## A SPIRIT-FILLED COMMUNITY

IN the discussion of the Book of Acts, it was observed that
the real hero of that book is the Holy Spirit of God. This
preëminent importance of the Spirit is one of the distinctive notes of the entire New Testament period. For men of
the apostolic age, the Church was no mere human society

159

for the propagation of a certain philosophy of life. It was the actual sphere in which God's Holy Spirit was at work. The Holy Spirit was not, of course, something different from God Himself. It was God, God in action. The God of the New Testament Church, like the God of the Old Testament, was a living God, never a pale philosophical abstraction or merely a necessary idea. The Christians of apostolic times knew that God had been at work *in Christ, reconciling the world unto himself (II Corinthians 5:19)*; they found that same God at work in their own midst, doing the works that Christ had done, healing the sick, transforming the lives of ordinary men, making saints out of sinners and heroes out of cowards. This present work of God in His Church they ascribed to the Holy Spirit, although they did not always carefully distinguish it from the work of Christ Himself. They were not concerned, in the excitement of the times, to formulate precise definitions. The experience was too new and fresh a thing for such analysis to seem necessary. Later Christian ages, on the basis of this experience would eventually provide a satisfactory intellectual statement of the relationships within the Godhead by the doctrine of the Trinity, but the experience itself was enough for the men of the New Testament. For them, as for us, the primary fact was that the remarkable things which were taking place in the Church were truly *the wonderful works of God (Acts 2:11)*.

### LIFE IN CHRIST MEANT LIFE IN THE CHURCH

To become a Christian has never meant merely to adopt a new set of beliefs or even to accept a new standard of conduct. It has always involved at least two things: first, a willingness, in faith and trust, to accept Christ as Lord; and second, to become a member of His Church. In New Testament times those who had accepted Christ as Lord were convinced that in doing so they had undergone an experience equivalent to passing from death into life *(St. John 5:24)*. The Christian believed that he had come to share in the very nature of Jesus Christ. He had become united to Him in a kind of mystical union so intense that he could say with Paul, *I live, yet not I, but Christ liveth in me (Galatians 2:20)*. So strong was the certainty of having found a new life in Christ that the relationship of Christians to Him could best be described in biological terms. Christ was the vine; they were the branches *(St. John 15:5)*. Or, to use an even more striking image, He was the body, they were the members. *For we are members of his body, of his flesh and his bones (Ephesians 5:30)*.

Obviously, people who used this kind of imagery could not be thinking of Christianity merely in terms of individual salvation. The character of their relationship to Christ involved a close relationship to other Christians. Christ's body had many members. Salvation could not be merely personal; it must be corporate. In finding redemption for himself, the Christian of necessity became the member of a redeemed and redemptive community.

The Christian of New Testament times knew that his life as a follower of Christ was life in the Church. The Church was the society of the New Covenant which Jesus had come to establish. It is called by many names in the New Testament: it is *the Church of the living God, the pillar and ground of the truth (I Timothy 3:15); the body of Christ (I Corinthians 12:27; Ephesians 1:22, 23, etc.);*

*the Israel of God (Galatians 6:16); the fellowship of the mystery (Ephesians 3:9)* and, by implication, *the bride of Christ (Ephesians 5:23).* This society was the authentic successor to the old national Israel. In it the mission of Israel was finally realized and all mankind brought within the covenant community of God, for membership in it was no longer restricted by race, nationality, or social status *(Galatians 3:28).* Christians were to love the Jews as members of God's ancient chosen people who still had a great destiny to fulfill *(Romans 9-11),* but the Jews as a nation had ceased to be the privileged people. They were regarded merely as *Israel after the flesh (I Corinthians 10:18);* those who belonged to the Church were the true Israel, *the children of promise (Galatians 3:29).*

### HOW ONE BECAME A CHURCH MEMBER: BAPTISM

THIS New Israel, like the old, had its appointed ordinances, its officers, and its common life. As time went on, these things were greatly elaborated, but even in the New Testament the main lines of the later development were already laid down. There was, first of all, a ceremony of initiation, the rite of baptism. At the very beginning of the Christian's life, its corporate character was emphasized. The experience of becoming a Christian was no mere individual matter. It was not enough to have accepted Christ as Lord in the privacy of one's heart, as though such a confession concerned the individual soul and God alone. As in the case of St. Paul, the first step after conversion was the public acknowledgment of one's faith and a formal incorporation into the fellowship of Christians by receiving the waters of baptism *(Acts 9:18).* To the early

Church, baptism was not, of course, merely an empty ceremony, but an effective sacramental means by which an individual was brought into a direct and personal relation with Jesus Christ and made to share in some mysterious way in His death and resurrection. *Know ye not, that so many of us as were baptized into Jesus Christ were baptized into his death? Therefore we are buried with him by baptism into death: that like as Christ was raised from the dead by the glory of the Father, even so we should also walk in newness of life (Romans 6:3, 4).* By baptism, which set the divine seal upon his personal act of faith, the believer came actually to participate in Christ's life. He was in Christ and Christ was in him. Faith and baptism were both necessary to accomplish this; the act of the individual and the act of the Church. Thus anyone who felt faith stirring within him requested first of all that he might be baptized and received into the Christian fellowship *(Acts 8:36-38).*

## HOW THE CHURCH WORSHIPPED: THE LORD'S SUPPER

THE newly baptized Christian found himself the member of a society of men deeply conscious of their relation to each other and of the responsibility of all for each. As members of Christ's Body, they knew that His life flowed through them all and that they were therefore members of each other *(Ephesians 4:25; I Corinthians 12:12-26).* There was an intimacy to their common life which was partly lost when the Church later became larger and more prosperous, but there has never been a time when this New Testament sense of community has entirely disappeared. The center of life for the New Testament Church was

163

the weekly assembly for worship and fellowship. Many of the early Jewish Christians continued to take part in the worship of the Old Israel in the Temple and the synagogue *(Acts 2:46)*, and to observe the Sabbath on the seventh day as prescribed in the Jewish Law. As the membership of the Church became increasingly Gentile and the full implications of the Gospel were realized, this double loyalty ceased and Christians came to worship with Christians alone. Instead of observing the Sabbath on the seventh day of the week, Christians began a new custom of meeting together for worship on the first day of the week, the day of Christ's resurrection from the dead. This day came to be called the Lord's Day *(Revelation 1:10)* and was celebrated joyfully as befitted a day which was a weekly Easter.

The most important event of the Lord's Day was the celebration of the Lord's Supper *(Acts 20:7)*. To the early Church this observance lay at the very heart of its life, as we can see from a description of the Church in Jerusalem. *They continued steadfastly in the apostles' doctrine and fellowship, and in the breaking of bread and of prayers (Acts 2:42).* In Paul's first epistle to the Corinthians *(11:17-34)* he gives a picture of the way in which the Eucharist would be celebrated in one of these New Testament churches. There were, of course, no church buildings, and the services would, of necessity, be held in private houses, probably in the home of one of the more well-to-do members of the congregation, since it would have to be large enough to hold a considerable crowd. The Lord's Supper was not an entirely separate service as it is with us, but part of a common meal to which apparently everyone brought his own food. This custom of the fellowship meal or love-feast, beautiful and appropriate though it was, later died out, partly as a result of abuses which can already be seen in Paul's description of the way in which it was conducted in the Corinthian Church. At some point in the meal, the elder or bishop blessed some of the bread and wine in imitation of our Lord's act at the Last Supper and all those present thankfully received of that which he had blessed. At each such celebration the sacrifice of Christ became a present fact *(ye do show the Lord's death till he come)* and the communicants became partakers of *the body and blood of the Lord.* In this service was gathered up the whole meaning of Christian fellowship, participation in a common source of strength and the expression of that participation in the living of a common life.

At these services and perhaps on other occasions, there was a place for prayers, for the reading of Scripture and for the singing of hymns. Psalms would be used as well as new Christian hymns which were beginning to appear *(Colossians 3:16).* There would on some occasions be a formal address or sermon by the bishop or elder in charge of the church, or by some visiting apostle who happened to be passing through. This would sometimes be an exposition of a passage of the Old Testament Scriptures (the only Bible which the early Christians had), or a stirring declaration concerning some aspect of the saving work of Christ, or a homily upon an ethical theme. The Epistle of James is a good example of this latter type of preaching. The New Testament churches were much more informal than the churches of later times became and there was always an opportunity for individual members of the congregation to take special part in it also. This occurred quite spontaneously and such participation might take the form of brief sermons or expositions, or prayers and hymns, or even of highly emotional utterances which expressed the feelings of the speaker although they were unintelligible to others, the so-called speaking with tongues. One can imagine that this excessive informality might lead to great confusion. It often did so and Paul, in writing to the Church at Corinth *(I Corinthians 14)*, had to put some curbs upon it in order to make sure that all things were done *decently and in order*. Whatever else may be said about worship in New Testament times, it was certainly not dull! Anyone attending the public assemblies of the Church would have been struck by a feeling of contagious enthusiasm and exuberant vitality.

### HOW THE CHURCH WAS ORGANIZED: THE MINISTRY

THE new Christian community, like the Old Israel, needed an organized ministry to carry on its affairs, to give authoritative instruction and to conduct the services of public worship. In the beginning, this organization was much looser than it later became and the technical terms used to describe it in the New Testament are not always used in the same sense they have today. Nevertheless, the main outlines of the familiar three-fold ministry are clearly to be seen. At the top, charged with special authority to govern the Church, were those who were called apostles. These included the original twelve, but also some others, like Paul, who were added to the number later. In general, these correspond to the bishops of the Church in later times, although they did not have the same kind of geographical jurisdiction. They had the power of ordination *(Acts 14:23)* and were regarded as, in some sense, the center of authority in the Church. In charge of the local congregations there were men called sometimes elders and sometimes bishops. The Greek word for elder is *presbyter* or as we say today, priest. The Greek word for bishop is *episcopos* and means merely overseer. It was originally applied to those who had the oversight of local congregations rather than to those with broader authority. Finally there was a third group of men who had charge of the practical matter of administering the charitable funds of the churches and of taking care of the poor *(Acts 6:1-8)*. These were called deacons, a term derived from a Greek word which means servant *(I Timothy 3:8-13)*. There also were other types of ministries in the apostolic period *(I Corinthians 12:28)*, but the relation of these ministries to the later ministry of the Church is not clear. At any rate they disappear in the following age. There was also, in New Testament times, a recognized order of devout women, the widows of I Timothy 5:3-10, which was the prototype of the orders of deaconesses and sisters in the later Church.

### HOW CHRISTIANS LIVED TOGETHER

THE existence of the orders of deacons and widows, charged with special responsibility for the poor and afflicted, calls attention to a striking feature of life in the New Testament Church: its sense of social responsibility for its members. This was a practical expression of that feeling which they all had of sharing a common life in Christ. The weekly celebration of the Lord's Supper was a constant reminder of this aspect of the Church's life. In the Jerusalem Church, the sense of communal responsibility was so strong that a large part of the membership adopted the practice of holding all their property in common. *All that believed were together and had all things common, and sold their possessions and goods and distributed them to all as every man had need (Acts 2:44, 45).* Nor was this spirit of mutual helpfulness limited to the members of individual congregations, but was felt by particular churches toward other churches. So Paul took up a collection among the churches of Greece for the impoverished mother church at Jerusalem during a time of famine *(I Corinthians 16:1-3).* One of the greatest of New Testament words is the Greek word *koinonia* which is translated in different places fellowship, communion, communication, and distribution, but always implies the thought of sharing, sharing in a common life, and sharing in the common responsibility of the group for all its members. The basic ethical principle of this early Christian fellowship is expressed in the words of Paul, *Bear ye one another's burdens and so fulfill the law of Christ (Galatians 6:2).*

Thus from the beginning, Christianity was not merely a way of individual salvation; it was a way of life which could be followed only within the framework of a social organism, the Christian Church. Within this Divine Society, which was the Body of Christ, the individual Christian learned the meaning of the law of love, that love which puts God and His eternal purposes at the center of life, and which exalts the permanent good of all above the selfish and temporary interests of individuals. It was also the conviction of Christians that this manner of life was intended ultimately to be a pattern for the ordering of the whole of human society.

## GREAT LETTERS OF THE APOSTOLIC CHURCH

THE epistles which, with the exception of one book, Revelation, make up the rest of the New Testament, can be understood fully only as one sees them against the background of the particular situation to which they are addressed. In this section it is impossible to give more than a brief account of the circumstances which produced each epistle and to state as concisely as possible the principal themes which the writer develops. In order to clothe this skeletal outline with flesh and blood, the reader will have to read the epistles for himself. For more detailed discussion of the background and of the meaning of individual passages, the reader is referred to the numerous Introductions to the New Testament and to commentaries on the various books.

### THE LETTERS OF PAUL

GREATEST of all the New Testament letters is the EPISTLE TO THE ROMANS written by Paul on his third missionary journey and addressed to the Church at Rome in order to prepare the way for a visit which he expected some day to undertake. Paul wanted the Roman Christians to understand his interpretation of the Christian Gospel and so took far more care in the preparation of this letter than was the case with any of the others. It is one of the most profound and influential documents in all the literature of the world, and deserves the most thoughtful kind of study, though much of it is admittedly difficult to understand without the aid of a teacher or a commentary. The basic argument, which is presented in chapters 1-8, is that salvation comes to men only through faith in Christ, not through any sort of personal achievement nor by mere obedience to any set of laws, whether ceremonial or moral. This is the doctrine of justification by faith alone. By faith Paul means, not just belief, nor the mere intellectual acceptance of a set of propositions, but personal commitment in a relationship of love, trust, and obedience. This part of the epistle reaches a magnificent climax in the eighth chapter. Some of the argument in the preceding chapters is hard to follow and there have been those who have dismissed Paul as a mere academic theologian on the basis of them. That is quite unjust. Suddenly, in this chapter, we realize the tremendous driving power of his faith, when he breaks out into something very close to poetry, *If God be for us, who can be against us? . . . For I am persuaded that neither death, nor life, nor angels, nor principalities, nor powers, nor things present, nor things to come, nor height, nor depth, nor any other creature, shall be able to separate us from the love of God which is in Christ Jesus our Lord (8:31-39).* The triumphant affirmation which these words contain is not something irrelevant to the preceding argument, but the direct consequence of it. Paul's sense of victory springs from the kind of relationship to God through faith in Christ which he has been describing in the previous chapters. Though these are perhaps the most difficult chapters in the New Testament, there are none which bring us closer to the real heart of the Christian Gospel. In chapters 9-11, Paul introduces a digression in which he discusses the vexing question, Why did the Jews not receive their own Messiah? and comes to the conclusion that their apparent apostasy is a necessary part of God's plan for the ultimate salvation of all mankind. From chapter 12 on, he describes the kind of moral life which is the inevitable outgrowth of a saving faith in Christ. The word *therefore* at the beginning of chapter 12 shows how closely related these ethical chapters are to the theological discussion in chapters 1-8. Because Christians have been brought near to God by their faith in Christ, they must offer themselves, their souls and bodies, to Him *to be a reasonable, holy, and living sacrifice*. The practical evidence of this, Paul says, will be a life which is pervaded by love, for *love is the fulfilling of the law (13:10)*. Next to the Sermon on the Mount these chapters contain the finest account of the Christian life to be found anywhere.

The two letters to the CORINTHIANS, in contrast to Romans, were written to a church Paul had founded and knew intimately. They are warm and human documents, sometimes affectionate, sometimes angry, and give us an unequaled picture of life in one of the new churches of the apostolic age. The first epistle was written in Ephesus during Paul's two-year stay at that city, located just across the Aegean Sea from Corinth, and was intended as a formal answer to the questions contained in a letter which he had received from the Corinthian Christians *(7:1)*. Before he began to answer their questions, however, he rebuked the Corinthians for some scandals and irregularities in their church. These were things he had learned about from friends who had recently visited him *(1:11)*. He was especially concerned about the way they had allowed themselves to become divided into factions *(1:10–4:21)*. Some were calling themselves disciples of Paul and some, disciples of Peter, while others considered themselves followers of Apollos, one of Paul's successors as spiritual leader of the Corinthian Church. The chief quarrel was over the merits of Paul and Apollos, and Paul rebukes them severely for disloyalty to Christ, for both Paul and Apollos are merely his ministers *(4:1)*. He then goes on to reprimand them further for the complacency with which they tolerate gross immorality and unbrotherly conduct in their midst *(5, 6)*. These Corinthian Christians were only a few years removed from paganism and Paul felt that they needed to be dealt with by a rod when love and gentleness failed to move them *(4:21)*. After he has dealt with these matters, Paul goes on to answer the inquiries which had occasioned their letter to him. There were, first of all, certain important questions about marriage (7) and the scruples which some felt about eating food which had been offered in the worship of idols *(8:10)*. This last was a very real concern for Christians who were living in a pagan environment and could not shut themselves off from daily contact and social intercourse with the pagan world. Paul's solution of the problem is one which commends itself to common sense and illustrates his gifts as a practical administrator and pastor *(10:23–11:1)*.

In the next section Paul discusses certain questions which had arisen about the manner of their common worship *(11:14)*. In connection with this he expounds the Christian doctrine of the Eucharist *(11:17-27; see also 10:16, 17)*. It is an interesting illustration of the genius of the New Testament, and indeed of the whole Bible, that this important doctrinal passage was written only because the things it contained seemed to have direct bearing upon a particular, concrete situation. Biblical doctrine always emerges as an answer to the problems of real life; never from a mere love of theorizing for its own sake. In this same context Paul sets down his great hymn in praise of Christian love. Some of the Corinthians were very proud of what they considered to be their great spiritual gifts and argued with each other as to the respective value of "speaking with tongues," "prophesying," "healing," and the like (12). Paul assures them that, great as all these gifts are, there is one that is infinitely greater, the gift of love, which alone can make a man acceptable to God (13:1-3). The epistle closes with an account of the Christian doctrine of the resurrection, which contains the earliest narrative of our Lord's resurrection appearances (15), and with some personal instructions and greetings (16).

The second epistle to the Corinthians was written some time later while Paul was traveling in Macedonia. In this epistle Paul is much more discursive than in the first, and the development of his thought is not so easy to follow. The main theme in the first part of the letter is a defense of his own conduct and apostleship (1-7). Great as Paul became, and deserved to become, in the eyes of the later Church, he had to fight a continual battle for recognition during his lifetime. His enemies accused him of not being really an apostle, and of being alternately arrogant and cringing toward other Christians (10:10). On this occasion they had accused him especially of fickleness because he had had to make some changes in his travel plans (1:15-17). In the first part of the epistle Paul's chief concern is to defend himself against these detractors. His thought, however, leads him naturally to discuss the nature of the Gospel ministry which he believed himself to share. The whole of chapters 3:1–7:4 is given over to this theme. *We are ambassadors for Christ,* he says, *God making his appeal through us (5:20 RSV). What we preach is not ourselves, but Jesus Christ as Lord, with ourselves as your servants for Jesus' sake (4:5, RSV).* This part of the epistle is followed by a kind of Every Member Canvass letter *(8, 9)* in which Paul appeals for contributions to a collection he is raising for the impoverished Church at Jerusalem, and in which he makes use of some of the subtle devices to awaken the interest and response of his readers which we fondly imagine to be the special discovery of modern advertising psychology.

In the concluding chapters *(10-13)* Paul returns even more vigorously to a defense of his right to be an apostle and gives some interesting and valuable information about his own adventurous career *(for example, 11:22-33).* Most scholars believe these last four chapters are really a separate letter written earlier than the rest of the book and perhaps are the very letter referred to in chapter 2:4. It would certainly make II Corinthians easier to understand if this were the case.

The EPISTLE TO THE GALATIANS is a passionately angry letter written to defend Paul's conception of the Gospel as a message which demands nothing from the believer but personal faith in Christ against those who insisted that Gentile Christians must become fully subject to the Jewish Law. It probably dates from about the same period as Romans to which its thought is very closely related. *For freedom,* he says, *did Christ set us free; stand fast therefore and be not entangled again in a yoke of slavery (5:1).*

Many scholars, for reasons impossible to discuss here, believe that EPHESIANS was written by a disciple of Paul, in the name of his master, as a kind of résumé of his teaching. Others, however, accept it as a genuine Pauline letter, in which case it is to be numbered among those letters written during his imprisonment in Rome *(3:1).* This epistle is most notable for its highly developed doctrine of the Church, which it calls the Body of Christ *(1:23, 5:30-32; see also 4:4, 5).* Using another striking figure, it compares the relationship between the Church and Christ to the relationship between a woman and her husband *(5:23-32).*

PHILIPPIANS was written to the first church which Paul had founded in Europe, to thank the members for their kindness to him during his imprisonment. It is important theologically for the doctrine concerning the person of Christ set forth in a passage which sounds like a fragment of an early Christian creed or hymn *(2:5-11).* It is the most serene and gracious of the letters and shows the character of Paul on its most attractive side.

COLOSSIANS, also written while Paul was in prison, was intended to warn the church at Colosse in Asia Minor against certain forms of Gnostic heresy which were already beginning to take root *(2:8).* There are very many close parallels between this epistle and that to the Ephesians, particularly in the conception of the Church as the Body of Christ *(1:24).* Incidental to his discussion of heresy, Paul sets forth a high theological conception of the nature of Christ, *who is the image of the invisible God, the first born of every creature,* by whom *were all things created, that are in heaven, and that are in earth (1:15, 16).*

First THESSALONIANS was probably the earliest of Paul's letters and if so, was the first book of the New Testament to be written. It was written from Corinth where Paul had just learned from his young friend Timothy that the Church at Thessalonica, one of the first churches he had founded in Europe *(Acts 17:1)* was still faithful to him and to the Gospel he had preached. The epistle is a spontaneous outpouring of gratitude for their fidelity *(3:6-9).* Paul also attempts to answer in this letter some questions which were troubling the Thessalonian Christians about the coming of the last day *(4:13–5:11).* Some members of the Church had died since Paul preached in Thessalonica, and the others were worried for fear that these departed members would have no part in the glorious day when the Lord came to receive His own. Paul reassures them by telling them that those who remain alive in that day will have no special advantage, for *the dead in Christ shall rise first (4:15, 16).* Although no one knows when that day will come, yet all Christians should live as though it were immediately at hand *(5:1-8).*

As often happens, his teaching in this first letter was misunderstood and the second epistle was written a few weeks later to correct the misunderstanding to which the first had given rise. Some of the Thessalonians had apparently understood Paul to mean in the first letter that the return of Christ was actually just about to happen and were giving up their jobs and their normal manner of life in expectation of it. In consequence, the life of the community was being seriously disrupted. In the second letter

176

Paul explains that there are certain mysterious events which must first occur and that Christians should continue to engage in their ordinary occupations *(2:1-5)*. If people will not work, then they shall not eat *(3:10)*! Both epistles illustrate Paul's great capacity for human affection and his profound common sense.

The three so-called Pastoral Epistles, I-II TIMOTHY and TITUS, are commonly regarded today as belonging to a much later age than that of Paul. The vocabulary, style, and ideas are so different from the authentic letters of Paul that it is an almost inevitable conclusion that they were written in the form of Pauline letters by an anonymous writer in order to show how he believed Paul would have dealt with the problems which arose in the Church after the second century had begun. They are concerned very largely with practical matters of church discipline and administration, hence the name, pastoral epistles. They are very valuable for the insight they give into the thought and life of the second century Church.

The letter to PHILEMON is a beautiful and kindly little note which Paul wrote in order to commend a runaway slave, Onesimus, to a friendly reception by his master, the Philemon of the title. Though Paul must have written many such, this is the only example of a Pauline letter which is concerned with individuals rather than with churches.

### THE LETTER TO THE HEBREWS

THE EPISTLE TO THE HEBREWS was included among the Pauline letters only by accident, as it nowhere claims to have been written by Paul, is very different in style and thought to the mind of Paul, and was generally recognized in the early Church as an anonymous letter. It is, as a matter of fact, not even in the form of a letter except for the concluding verses. It is rather a formal essay, or perhaps a sermon, which endeavors to show by using an allegorical[1] interpretation of certain Old Testament passages, in what way the work of Christ was a fulfilment of the Jewish priestly and sacrificial system. Christ is the true priest and his sacrifice the one true sacrifice. The emotional climax of the epistle is reached in the eleventh chapter with its stirring account of the men of old who lived amidst the hardships of this present world by virtue of their indomitable faith in the realities of the unseen world. The author's practical purpose was to stimulate his readers, whoever they were, perhaps the Christians at Rome, to show a like faith and to stand firm in the face of imminent persecution *(12:1-11)*.

### LETTERS BY OTHER NEW TESTAMENT PERSONALITIES

THE name of JAMES, *the Lord's brother (Galatians 1:19)* and leader of the conservative Jewish faction in the early Church, is appropriately attached to the little homily, or collection of homilies, on Christian morality which goes under his name, whether he was the author of it or not. It is more Jewish in spirit and contains less of distinctively Christian doctrine than any other New Testament book. That is in no way to depreciate it, since it is an excellent example of the kind of practical moral teaching which

---

[1] Allegorical method, a system of interpretation, common among Greek-speaking Jews of that day, which was concerned with the spiritual meaning believed to underlie the obvious literal meaning of Biblical passages.

must have accompanied always the triumphant proclamation of the good news about Christ. It is particularly notable for its sympathy with the social underdog *(5:1-6)*.

Of the two epistles of PETER, the second was commonly denied to be the work of the apostle even in the early Church and is largely a rewriting of the little epistle of JUDE. The main purpose of both Jude and second Peter is to attack heresy and to warn that, in spite of long delay, the day of the Lord is surely coming.

The first epistle, on the other hand, is still regarded by many competent scholars as an authentic work of Peter, the prince of the apostles, and is, in any case, one of the greatest books in the New Testament, written to encourage some group of Christians who were about to undergo persecution to be faithful and Christlike in their behaviour *(4:12-19)*.

It is still a disputed question whether the three epistles of JOHN were written by the author of the fourth Gospel or by a disciple of his. The question is largely academic because there can be no doubt that the spirit and general point of view are the same. The first epistle was written to warn the recipients against the Gnostic heresy known as docetism, which maintained that Christ's life and death were merely appearances and that He had not really come "in the flesh" *(4:1-3)*. Along with his principal theme, the author dwells upon the thought of love as the distinguishing mark of the Christian life and the most direct means of access to God *(4:7)*.

The same message is concisely contained in the second epistle, a brief note addressed by the Elder John to an unknown church, *the elect lady.* Third John is an equally brief personal note addressed to a certain Gaius, commending him for his hospitality toward some itinerant evangelists.

### A VISION OF GOD AND HIS KINGLY RULE: REVELATION

THE last book in the New Testament is, for many people, the most difficult, and has occasioned more misunderstanding and fantastic speculation than any other book in the Bible except Daniel. Both REVELATION and Daniel belong to a peculiar category of ancient religious literature called apocalyptic and one cannot understand them unless he understands what the apocalyptic writers were trying to do. The purpose of both Daniel and Revelation was to encourage their readers to remain steadfast in time of persecution; in the case of Revelation, the persecution of the Christians by the Emperor Domitian *c*. 95 A.D. The strange and occasionally repellent imagery of Revelation is simply a part of the traditional apocalyptic language and can be understood in detail only with the help of a Biblical commentary. One can read the book, however, with profit and interest if he will only remember that the author, an otherwise unknown prophet of Asia Minor whose name was John, is really writing poetry, not prose, and under all the confused images of his supernatural drama is trying to make vivid to his readers the one great truth that all history, both human and cosmic, is under the dominion of Almighty God and that those who trust and obey Him need have no fear however dark the human situation may seem to be. The thought of the entire work is summed up in the words, *The Lord God omnipotent reigneth* (*19:6*).

It is fitting that the last book in the Bible should have this thought for its basic theme. The Bible story begins with the creation of the world; it ends with a vision of the coming of the Kingdom of God. It was God who made the world and it is God who will bring it finally to perfection. The course of Biblical history, like the course of world history, sometimes seems devious and uncertain, but over it at every turning of the way presides the figure of One who is *the Alpha and Omega, the Faithful and True, the King of Kings and Lord of Lords (Revelation 1:8; 19:11, 16).*

## THE TRANSITION TO CHURCH HISTORY

As we close the last book of the New Testament, we have come to the end of the great creative and normative age of Christian history. What follows this is the history of the Church and adds nothing to the essential content of the Gospel. In a sense, of course, the whole of the Bible is a part of Church history, since it tells how and why the Church began and traces its development from its Jewish to its Christian form, but nevertheless there is a qualitative difference between the Biblical books which record the definitive acts of sacred history, and the writings of the age which followed. In the New Testament we see how the Gospel took shape and how the Church received the basic form which she would bear ever afterward. In the years which followed there would still be growth and development; men of brilliant spiritual and intellectual achievement would bring new insights to illuminate the meaning of the faith; the Church would adapt herself to new conditions in countries yet unknown and in centuries yet undreamed of; but the main lines within which that development would take place had already been laid down. The men of the sub-apostolic age were conscious that they were the guardians of something which had been entrusted to them; they were building upon a foundation already firmly laid. In some of the later and peripheral writings of the New Testament itself, we are already conscious of the emergence of this new spirit *(Jude 3; I Timothy 6:20)*, but what is only a rare exception in the New Testament becomes the dominant note of the age which follows. Which is only to say that in following our story beyond the limits of the New Testament, we move outside the sphere of Biblical Revelation into that of Church history, the subject of another volume in this series.

*The Word*
*Was Made*
*Flesh*

**PART FOUR**

Conclusion

# Christ the Word

THE Faith of the Church is founded upon
the Bible and the heart of the Bible is the Gospel of Jesus
Christ, the Good News that the promises given to ancient
Israel have been fulfilled. A Christian is one who believes
in this Gospel and accepts Christ in trust and obedience
as the Saviour and long-awaited Redeemer of the world.

The various aspects of the nature and redeeming work
of Christ are discussed in another volume in this series,
but here, while we are still dealing with the Biblical materials, we need to take note of one of His titles which,
more than any other, makes plain the unity and meaning
of the Bible story. This is the title given Him in the first
chapter of the fourth gospel: *The Word of God (St. John
1:1)*. As we have already seen (page 9), the Bible as a whole
is called the Word of God, and it may seem paradoxical
that the same phrase should be used to describe our Lord.
But it is just in this paradox that we see the inner co-

herence of the Bible most clearly. It will be remembered that *word* means message. It is the faith of Christians that in the person and work of Jesus Christ there is summed up the whole word or message of God found scattered through the rest of the Bible.

In the Old Testament, God's message appears little by little, emerging slowly over a long period of time, as men were able to grasp it. But, at the end of this process, *in the fullness of the time (Galatians 4:4)*, God revealed Himself completely and finally in Jesus Christ. As the prologue to the fourth Gospel says, *The Word became flesh and dwelt among us (St. John 1:4)*. What God had been trying to say to men in so many different ways and which they had understood so inadequately, He now says plainly and unmistakably through a Person; not a mere man, who could only *speak* of reconciliation between God and man, but one who was both God and Man, in whom that reconciliation actually took place; not a mere teacher, who could only *tell* of God's mighty acts, but One in whom the Godhead dwelt *(Colossians 2:9)* who could Himself perform them; not a mere prophet, who could only *say* the word, but God's only begotten Son, who is the Word. Jesus Christ sums up the whole of the previous revelation and supplies all that still was lacking. His life, death, and resurrection are the climax of the whole story. And, since we can understand the full meaning of any story only when we know how it ends, we can understand the whole of the preceding story in the Bible only when we see who He was and what He did. He who was the Word of God Incarnate gives us the key for understanding the Word of God contained in the rest of the Bible. Without Him, the rest of the story would be obscure and incomplete.

Furthermore, it is through Him that we see the direct relevance of the Bible to our own lives. For the Bible is not a book of good advice which touches us as individuals only indirectly and as we choose to let it; it is the story of a divine redemption in which we are directly and inescapably concerned. Christ is the center of the story and we who are members of His Church are part of that story and ourselves participants in the great drama of man's salvation. As we read the Bible story we come to understand how we, by our pride and self-love, have separated ourselves from God; but we also see how God, across the centuries, has endeavored to bridge the gulf which we have made. In Jesus Christ the gulf was bridged and the way of reconciliation opened. *As many as received him, to them gave he power to become the sons of God, even to them that believe on his name (St. John 1:12).* Because we have received Him, however ineffectually, our lives have been drawn into the stream of Biblical history.

Although the whole of the Bible story is important, yet clearly the story of Christ and His work is most important. As we read the Bible today we should read it with that knowledge and allow Him to cast His light on every page and show Himself as the unseen goal toward which even the most difficult chapters point. Our chief interest in reading the Bible should be to capture for ourselves the experience of the first generations of Christians who could say, in the words of the fourth Gospel, *we beheld his glory, the glory as of the only begotten of the father . . . and of his fullness have we received, and grace upon grace (St. John 1:14, 16).*

# APPENDIX

# Reading List

# Books for Reference

THE books included in this list are intended primarily for clergy, church school teachers, and interested lay people who may be desirous of more information about particular subjects than is contained in this book. Except where especially noted, the books in this list are not of a technical character and should be easily intelligible to the average educated layman. The inclusion of any book in this list does not imply necessarily approval of all its conclusions or even of its general point of view. Many books on the Bible are written by persons who do not sympathize with the general position of the Episcopal Church. Many are written from a purely literary or historical point of view without any consideration of the religious values of the Bible. Such books may contain valuable information and stimulating insights, but the reader must always be on guard against accepting uncritically what may be only the personal opinions of a particular author as the unquestioned conclusions of modern scholarship.

## GENERAL BOOKS ON THE MEANING AND AUTHORITY OF THE BIBLE

*A Preface to Bible Study* by Alan Richardson (Philadelphia: Westminster. 1944). Brief, readable, Christian, and theological in the best sense of the word.

191

*The Authority of the Biblical Revelation* by Hubert Cunliffe-Jones (Boston: Pilgrim. 1949). A brief, but serious, recent study of the problems involved.

*The Bible Today* by Charles Harold Dodd (Cambridge University Press. 1947). How God reveals Himself in history.

*The Relevance of the Bible* by Harold Henry Rowley (New York: Macmillan. 1944). A sane, persuasive discussion of the present value of the Bible.

*The Modern Use of the Bible* by Harry Emerson Fosdick (New York: Macmillan. [1924] 1947). The most popular book of its kind. The standpoint is that of Protestant liberalism.

*The Authority of the Scriptures* by John William Charles Wand (London: Mowbray. 1949). A popular treatment by the Bishop of London.

BOOKS WHICH SUGGEST HOW TO READ THE BIBLE

*A Guide Book to the Bible* by Alice Parmalee (New York: Harpers. 1948). A very useful book for the ordinary reader.

*How to Read the Bible* by Edgar Johnson Goodspeed (Philadelphia: Winston. 1946). A practical and reliable course of study outlined by a great scholar.

*An Introduction to the Bible* by Stanley Cook (Pelican Books). Contains a remarkable amount of information about Bible background and the contents of the individual books.

*The Bible and the Common Reader* by Mary Ellen Chase (New York: Macmillan. 1944). Deals with the Bible as great literature.

*A Guide for Bible Readers* by Harris Franklin Rall (Nashville: Abingdon-Cokesbury). A series of eight paper-bound volumes containing a complete course of reading in the Old and New Testaments with explanatory comments.

## GENERAL BOOKS ON THE RELIGIOUS IDEAS OF THE BIBLE

*An Outline of Biblical Theology* by Millar Burrow (Philadelphia: Westminster. 1946). Encyclopedic in scope but not difficult reading.

*A Guide to the Understanding of the Bible* by Harry Emerson Fosdick (New York: Harpers. 1938). Traces through the Bible the attempts to deal with life's basic issues. Chapters on the value of the individual, the meaning of suffering, the conception of God, etc.

*The Social Teaching of the Prophets and Jesus* by Charles Foster Kent (New York: Scribners. 1917).

192

*Our Bible and the Ancient Manuscripts* by Sir Frederic George Kenyon (New York: Harpers. 1940).

## GENERAL TOOLS FOR BIBLE STUDY

ANYONE who desires to penetrate beyond the surface in Bible study will need, in addition to a copy of the Bible with Apocrypha, a concordance, an atlas, and a one-volume Bible commentary. A dictionary of the Bible is also helpful.

### VERSIONS OF THE BIBLE

*The King James or Authorized Version.* Innumerable editions. The great classic English version. Because its Elizabethan style is in many places obscure to the modern reader and because recent scholarship has made it possible to translate many passages more accurately, it should be supplemented by the use of one of the revised versions and, if possible, by a modern translation.

*The (English) Revised Version.* English University Presses.

*The American Standard Version* (New York: Nelson). Closest of all versions to the original Greek and Hebrew.

*The Revised Standard Version* (New York: Nelson). More flowing and idiomatic in style than the American Standard Version. It may well become standard in fact as well as in name for American non-Roman Christianity. The Old Testament has not yet been published in this version.

### TRANSLATIONS OF THE BIBLE INTO MODERN SPEECH

*A New Translation of the Bible* by James Moffatt (New York: Harpers. [1922] 1935).

*The Complete Bible, An American Translation* by John Merlin Powis Smith and Edgar Johnson Goodspeed (Includes the Apocrypha) (Chicago: University of Chicago. 1939). *The Short Bible* is an abridged version of this translation, published in The Modern Library, 1933.

*The Holy Bible* by Ronald Knox (New York: Sheed and Ward. 3 vol. 1938). An authorized translation for Roman Catholics, written in a delightful English style. The arrangement of the Old Testament books is that of the Roman Catholic Church and the footnotes must be used with caution.

*The Westminster Historical Atlas to the Bible* by G. E. Wright and F. V. Filson (Philadelphia: Westminster). An indispensable book with beautiful maps, as well as a large store of recent and reliable information about the background of the Bible.

*The Historical Geography of the Holy Land* by George Adams Smith (London: Hodder and Stoughton. [1894] 1936). The great classic on the subject. Eminently readable and on the whole still reliable.

*The River Jordan* by Nelson Glueck (Philadelphia: Westminster. 1946). A delightful survey of the geography of the Jordan valley. Attractively illustrated.

## CONCORDANCES

*A Complete Concordance to the Holy Scriptures* by Alexander Cruden (New York: Revell). The standard work for the reader concerned only with the English text.

*Analytical Concordance to the Bible* by Robert Young (New York: Funk and Wagnalls. 1947). Either this or the following volume is necessary for the reader who knows Greek or Hebrew.

*The Exhaustive Concordance of the Bible* by James Strong (Nashville: Abingdon-Cokesbury).

*Complete Concordance of the American Standard Version* by Marshall Custiss Hazard (New York: Nelson. 1922).

## ONE-VOLUME BIBLE COMMENTARIES

*A Commentary on the Holy Bible* by John Robert Dummelow, edited by S. Parkes Cadman (New York: Macmillan. [1908] 1947). Good, but not up-to-date on many points.

*A New Commentary on Holy Scripture* by Charles Gore (New York: Macmillan. 1929). Written from a distinctly Anglican point of view; has the advantage of including a brief commentary on the Apocrypha.

*The Abingdon Bible Commentary* by Frederick Carl Eiselen (Nashville: Abingdon-Cokesbury. 1933). Somewhat more abreast of current scholarship than Gore.

*The Study Bible* (Philadelphia: Westminster). The text of the King James Version with introductions to the books and copious explanatory notes. A very useful volume.

## DICTIONARIES OF THE BIBLE

*The Westminster Dictionary of the Bible* edited by Henry Snyder Gehman (Philadelphia: Westminster. 1944). Conservative and reliable. Not as detailed as

*Dictionary of the Bible* edited by James Hastings. One-volume and five-volume editions (New York: Scribners). The one-volume edition is a different work, not a mere condensation of the five-volume edition. Both are standard works of reference.

*A Companion to the Bible* edited by Thomas Walter Manson (New York: Scribners. 1940). A large amount of significant information in convenient form.

### ARCHAEOLOGICAL AND CULTURAL BACKGROUND

*An Encyclopedia of Bible Life* by Madeline (Sweeny) and John Lane Miller (New York: Harpers. 1944). Full of fascinating information readily available nowhere else.

*Daily Life in Bible Times* by Albert Edward Bailey (New York: Scribners. 1943). Much briefer than the above and very readable.

*Light from the Ancient Past* by Jack Finegan (Princeton: University Press. 1947). A large and beautifully printed sketch of the principal archæological discoveries as they throw light on the Old and New Testaments and on the history of the early Church. Profusely illustrated.

*Archæology and the Bible* by George Aaron Barton (Philadelphia: American Sunday School Union. 1933). A standard reference work. Chiefly valuable as containing *verbatim* the principal ancient texts which bear on the Bible story.

*What Mean These Stones* by Millar Burrows (New Haven: American Schools of Oriental Research). A clear and scholarly book which describes the contributions made by recent archæology to various areas of Biblical study.

*Archæology and the Religion of Israel* by William Foxwell Albright (Baltimore: Johns Hopkins University Press. 1942). An important statement by the greatest authority on the subject of the revolutionary importance of archæology for evaluating the nature of Israel's religion.

*The Archæology of Palestine* by William Foxwell Albright (Pelican Books, 1949). Brief, interesting, authoritative, and inexpensive.

*A History of Hebrew Civilization* by Alfred Bertholet (New York: Brentano's. 1926). An excellent comprehensive survey of the life and culture of the ancient Hebrews.

*Ancient Near Eastern Texts Relating to the Old Testament* edited by James B. Pritchard (Princeton University Press. 1950). Very expensive, but monumental in scope and indispensable to the scholar.

# BOOKS DEALING WITH THE OLD TESTAMENT

## THE HISTORY OF ISRAEL

THERE are two large works which deal with the subject in a detailed and rather technical way: Oesterley and Robinson's *A History of Israel* (New York: Oxford. Two volumes) and A. Lods' two volumes *Israel from Its Beginning to the Middle of the Eighth Century* and *The Prophets and the Rise of Judaism* (New York: Knopf).

There are many briefer histories of which these are only a selection:

*The History and Religion of Israel* by William Landsell Wardle. Clarendon Bible, vol. I (New York: Oxford. 1936). Probably the best single volume for the intelligent Sunday school teacher or lay inquirer.

*Essentials of Bible History* by Elmer Wallace King Mould (New York: Nelson. 1939). Covers both the Old and New Testament periods.

*The Genius of Israel* by Carleton Eldredge Noyes (Boston: Houghton-Mifflin. 1924). Contains not only the essential facts but a real appreciation of their meaning.

*Old Testament History* by Ismar John Peritz (Nashville: Abingdon-Cokesbury. 1915).

*Old Testament History* by Henry Preserved Smith (New York: Scribners. 1903).

*History of the Hebrew People* and *History of the Jewish People* by Charles Foster Kent (New York: Scribners). A whole generation of Protestant Christians was raised on these standard and instructive works.

## INTRODUCTION TO THE LITERATURE OF THE OLD TESTAMENT

*Introduction to the Old Testament* by Robert Henry Pfeiffer (New York: Harpers. 1941). This is an extremely technical work which would not be of interest to the ordinary layman and is probably too detailed to be especially useful to the average clergyman. It is definitely a work for specialists and, in this field, has largely taken the place once held by S. R. Driver's *Introduction to the Literature of the Old Testament.*

The following are less technical and better suited to the needs of the average priest and lay person:

*The Old Testament, Its Making and Meaning* by Henry Wheeler Robinson (Nashville: Abingdon-Cokesbury). The best book for a rapid survey of the contents of the Old Testament. It might well be read in conjunction with L. B. Longacre's *The Old Testament, Its Form and Purpose* (same publishers) which describes how the Old Testament was written and how it came to have its present form.

*Introduction to the Books of the Old Testament* by William Oscar Emil Oesterley and T. H. Robinson (New York: Macmillan. 1934).

*Introduction to the Old Testament* by John Edgar MacFadyen (London: Hodder and Stoughton. [1932] 1947).

*The Story of the Old Testament* by Edgar Johnson Goodspeed (Chicago: University of Chicago Press. 1934). Brief and easy to read.

*The Literature of the Old Testament* by George Foot Moore (New York: Holt. Home University Library. [1913] 1948).

*A Critical Introduction to the Old Testament* by George Buchanan Gray (New York: Scribners. 1913).

*Literature of the Old Testament in Its Historical Development* by Julius August Bewer (New York: Columbia University. 1922). This is a different kind of book from those mentioned immediately above since it discusses the literature in a coherent narrative style in the order in which the various parts of the Old Testament were written. It is widely used as a college textbook.

*The Hebrew Literary Genius* by Duncan Black MacDonald (Princeton: University Press. 1933). A fresh and attractive discussion of the thought world of the ancient Hebrews and their literary methods. (Not an introduction in the sense in which the term is used above, but a good antidote to the fragmentary approach which such books must necessarily use.)

COLLECTIONS OF ESSAYS ON VARIOUS OLD TESTAMENT SUBJECTS

*Record and Revelation* edited by Henry Wheeler Robinson (New York: Oxford. 1938). An excellent collection of essays summarizing the conclusions of recent scholarship on such subjects as the History and Religion of Israel, Old Testament Theology, Archæology, Language, etc.

*The People and the Book* edited by Arthur Samuel Peake (New York: Oxford. 1926). An older, but still valuable collection, similar to the above.

THE RELIGION OF THE OLD TESTAMENT

THE approach to this subject may be made from two directions: that of the chronological growth of Israel's religion and that of a general survey of the great religious ideas of the Old Testament. The latter approach is generally called Old Testament Theology. Both approaches are necessary for a real understanding of the subject.

*The Theology of the Old Testament* by Otto Justice Baab (Nashville: Abingdon-Cokesbury. 1949). The only thoroughly up-to-date treatise on the subject.

*Outline of Old Testament Theology* by Charles Fox Burney (New York: Gorham). Oxford Church Text Book Series. An excellent brief manual.

*The Religious Ideas of the Old Testament* by Henry Wheeler Robinson (New York: Scribners. 1913).

*The Religious Teaching of the Old Testament* by Albert Cornelius Knudson (Nashville: Abingdon-Cokesbury. 1918).

*The Distinctive Ideas of the Old Testament* by Norman Henry Snaith (Philadelphia: Westminster. 1944). Solid reading. Chiefly for the clergy.

*Israel, Its Life and Culture* by Johannes Pedir Eiler Pedersen (New York: Oxford. 1946). An exhaustive study in four volumes of the psychology and world view of the Hebrews.

These books are all histories of Israel's Religion:

*Hebrew Religion* by William Oscar Emil Oesterley and Robinson (New York: Macmillan, 1937). A standard work, but tends rather to over-emphasize the primitive features in Hebrew religion at the expense of its distinctive character.

*The Religious Pilgrimage of Israel* by I. G. Matthews (New York: Harpers. 1947). The most recent and one of the most elaborate, but written from a thoroughly humanistic point of view.

*Old Testament Religion* by Elmer Archibald Leslie (Nashville: Abingdon-Cokesbury. 1936). Interesting for its use of recent discoveries about the religion of the Canaanites.

*The Religion of the People of Israel* by Rudolf Kittel (New York: Macmillan. 1925). Brief, conservative, easily read.

*Revelation and Response in the Old Testament* by Cuthbert Aikman Simpson (New York: Columbia. 1947). The development of Hebrew religious thought to the Exile. Makes much use of Toynbee's philosophy of history.

*The Religion of Israel* by George Aaron Barton (Philadelphia: University of Pennsylvania. 1928).

*The Religion of Israel* by Henry Preserved Smith (New York: Scribners. 1914).

*The Religion of Israel* by John Punnett Peters (Boston: Ginn).

All three of the above are now somewhat antiquated. In this connection also, mention should be made of Wardle's *The History and*

*Religion of Israel* which is listed above under histories of Israel. The latter half of this useful little book gives a brief survey of the religion.

### PERSONALITIES OF THE OLD TESTAMENT

*Great Men and Movements in Israel* by Rudolf Kittel (New York: Macmillan. 1929). An interesting and readable account of the great characters who move across the pages of the Old Testament.

*Personalities of the Old Testament* by Fleming James (New York: Scribners. 1939). A large, but eminently readable account of the Old Testament in terms of its great figures. One of the best books to read for a general introduction to the Hebrew Scriptures.

### THE RELIGIOUS VALUE OF THE OLD TESTAMENT

*The Rediscovery of the Old Testament* by Harold Henry Rowley (Philadelphia: Westminster. 1946). A recent and attractive account of the significance of the Old Testament for the contemporary world, which also contains a good deal of information about archæology and other subjects.

*The Authority of the Old Testament* by Arthur Gabriel Hebert (New York: Morehouse-Gorham. 1947). Almost required reading for the clergy and educated lay people.

*The Throne of David* by Arthur Gabriel Hebert (New York: Morehouse-Gorham. 1942). A Christological approach to the Old Testament. A good example of contemporary theological study of the Bible, but can be recommended only with reserve because of the author's sympathy toward allegorical exegesis.

*The People and the Presence* by William John Telia Phythian-Adams (New York: Oxford. 1942). This and numerous other works by the same author are interesting and contain many stimulating insights, but should be read with considerable caution, as the majority of Old Testament scholars would regard many of the author's conclusions as fanciful in the extreme.

*The Challenge of Israel's Faith* by George Ernest Wright (Chicago: University Press. 1944). A stimulating account of the prophetic strain in the religion of Israel, somewhat tinged with neo-orthodox theology.

### BOOKS ON THE PROPHETS

*The Goodly Fellowship of the Prophets* by John Paterson (New York: Scribners. 1948). A very readable recent account covering all the prophetic books.

*The Prophets and Their Times* by John Merlin Powis Smith revised by W. A. Irwin (Chicago: University Press. 1941). Good except for the chapter on Ezekiel, which embodies Irwin's own peculiar views.

*The Prophets Tell Their Own Story* by Elmer Archibald Leslie (Nashville: Abingdon-Cokesbury. 1939).

*Prophecy and the Prophets in Ancient Israel* by Theodore Henry Robinson (New York: Scribners).

*Beacon Lights of Prophecy* by Albert Cornelius Knudson (Nashville: Abingdon-Cokesbury. 1914).

*The Prophetic Movement in Israel* by Albert Cornelius Knudson (Nashville: Abingdon-Cokesbury. 1921). A brief, popular account intended primarily for lay groups.

*The Relevance of the Prophets* by Robert Belgarnie Young Scott (New York: Macmillan. 1944). This and the following book give a cross-section of the prophetic world of thought, rather than a history of the prophetic movement.

*Prophetic Religion* by James Philip Hyatt (Nashville: Abingdon-Cokesbury. 1947).

### THE POETIC AND WISDOM LITERATURE

*The Poetry of the Old Testament* by Theodore Henry Robinson (London: Duckworth. 1948). The best comprehensive treatment of the poetical books for the average reader.

*Israel's Wisdom Literature, Its Bearing on Theology and the History of Religion* by Oliver Shaw Rankin (New York: Scribners. 1936).

*The Wisdom Literature of the Old Testament* by William Theophilus Davison (London: Kelly).

*The Hebrew Literature of Wisdom in the Light of Today* by John Franklin Genung (Boston: Houghton-Mifflin. 1906).

### SPECIAL TOPICS IN OLD TESTAMENT RELIGION

*The Ethics of the Old Testament* by H. G. Mitchell (Chicago: University Press).

*The Moral Life of the Hebrews* by John Merlin Powis Smith (Chicago: University Press. 1923).

*The Origin and History of Hebrew Law* by John Merlin Powis Smith (Chicago: University Press. 1931).

*Sacrifices in Ancient Israel* by William Oscar Emil Oesterley (New York: Macmillan. 1937).

*A Critical History of the Doctrine of a Future Life* by Robert Henry Charles (New York: Macmillan).

*Immortality and the Unseen World* by William Oscar Emil Oesterley (New York: Macmillan. 1921).

*Israel's Hope of Immortality* by Charles Fox Burney (New York: Oxford).

*The Problem of Suffering in the Old Testament* by Arthur Samuel Peake (London: Bryant).

SEPARATE COMMENTARIES ON THE BOOKS OF THE OLD TESTAMENT

THERE are several series of commentaries which cover all or most of the Old Testament books. The various volumes of the *International Critical Commentary* (New York: Scribners) are too technical for all except specialists in Biblical study, though they may be useful for detailed reference on some particularly knotty problem of interpretation. The *Westminster Commentaries* (London: Methuen) are less technical and therefore more useful to the common reader. The series is far from complete. The ordinary lay person will probably find most help in the various small volumes of the *New Century Bible* (New York: Oxford) and the *Cambridge Bible for Schools and Colleges* (Cambridge: University Press). These two series are nearly complete. In the case of the Cambridge Bible, though, the reader must be careful to get the latest edition, as, in the case of many of the Old Testament books, the older editions are now antiquated. The series of small commentaries for lay people entitled *The Bible for Home and School* (New York: Macmillan) is rather old, but still useful where available. The series called the *Clarendon Bible* (New York: Oxford) is especially designed for the church school teacher and excellent of its type. It is attractively published and interesting to read. The chief defect is that it deals with only selected parts of the Old Testament. It does, however, cover most that is of primary significance. The separate volumes are: 1. *History and Religion of Israel*, 2. *From Moses to Elisha*, 3. *Decline and Fall of the Hebrew Kingdoms*, 4. *Israel After the Exile*, 5. *Judaism in the Greek Period*, 6. *In the Beginning* (a brief commentary on Genesis). The several volumes of C. F. Kent's *The Historical Bible* (New York: Scribners), although now old and dated in some particulars, still contain much that is valuable. The same holds true of the author's more elaborate *The Students Old Testament*. When the several volumes of *The Interpreters' Bible* (Nashville: Abingdon-Cokesbury) are issued, they will embody the latest scholarship and will prove a most useful source of reference.

The following list is restricted to the more important books of the Old Testament and the commentaries mentioned are in each case the best for general purposes of reference.

*The Book of Genesis* by Samuel Rolles Driver. Westminster Commentaries (New York: Gorham).

*In the Beginning* by Samuel Henry Hooke. Vol. VI. The Clarendon Bible (New York: Oxford).

*The Book of Exodus* by Samuel Rolles Driver. The Cambridge Bible for Schools and Colleges (New York: Macmillan).

*Deuteronomy and Joshua* by Henry Wheeler Robinson. The New Century Bible.

*The Book of Judges* by George Albert Cooke. Cambridge Bible for Schools and Colleges (New York: Macmillan).

*The Book of Judges* by C. F. Burney (New York: Macmillan). A much more technical work, intended for the specialist.

*I and II Samuel* by R. S. Kennedy. The New Century Bible.

*I and II Kings* by John Skinner. The New Century Bible.

*The Books of Ezra and Nehemiah* by Herbert Edward Ryle. Cambridge Bible for Schools and Colleges (New York: Macmillan).

*Job* by Arthur Samuel Peake. New Century Bible.

*The Book of Job* by Andrew Bruce Davidson. Cambridge Bible for Schools and Colleges (New York: Macmillan. 1918).

*The Cross of Job* by Henry Wheeler Robinson. Religion and Life Book (London: S. C. M. 1938).

*The Psalms* by Elmer Archibald Leslie (Nashville: Abingdon-Cokesbury. 1949). The latest book on the subject. Valuable because of its scope, but the reader should be aware that it is in part based upon theories as to the function of some of the psalms which are by no means universally accepted.

*Thirty Psalmists* by Fleming James (New York: Putnam. 1938). A readable account of thirty of the more important psalms.

*The Psalms* by A. F. Kirkpatrick. The Cambridge Bible for Schools and Colleges. Very old and completely outmoded in its general critical position, but still valuable for its genuine combination of learning with piety.

*The Psalms* by William Oscar Emil Oesterley (New York: Macmillan. 1938). A complete modern commentary on the psalms. Useful for bringing Kirkpatrick up-to-date.

*The Religion of the Psalms* by John Merlin Powis Smith (Chicago: University of Chicago).

*Proverbs* by William Oscar Emil Oesterley. Westminster Commentaries.

*Isaiah* by John Skinner. Two volumes. The Cambridge Bible for Schools and Colleges (New York: Macmillan).

*The Book of Isaiah* by Sir George Adam Smith. Two volumes. The Expositors Bible. A standard book of an older generation. Somewhat verbose, but still very useful (New York: Harpers, new rev. ed. 1928).

*Isaiah, His Life and Times* by Samuel Rolles Driver (New York: Revell). A good brief survey of the whole of the writings included under Isaiah's name.

*Event in Eternity* by Paul Ehrman Scherer (New York: Harpers. 1945). Not a commentary, but a suggestive homiletic treatment of Second Isaiah.

*The Cross of the Servant: A Study in Deutero-Isaiah* by Henry Wheeler Robinson (London: S. C. M.).

*Jeremiah* by Leonard Elliot Binns. Westminster Commentaries (New York: Gorham. 1919).

*Jeremiah the Prophet, A Study in Personal Religion* by Raymond Calkins (New York: Macmillan. 1930).

*Prophecy and Religion* by John Skinner (New York: Macmillan. 1936). Not a commentary, but a series of essays. The best book on Jeremiah, but not for the casual reader.

*The Cross of Jeremiah* by Henry Wheeler Robinson (London: S. C. M.).

*The Book of Ezekiel* by John Skinner. The Expositors Bible. A good treatment of the book from a conservative, critical point of view. The study of the book of Ezekiel is in a more confused state in present-day scholarship than that of any other prophetic book. The reader who is interested in getting some idea of the trend of more recent criticism will find a good example of it in the following volume.

*Ezekiel* by Isaac George Matthews (Philadelphia: American Baptist Publication Society. 1939). A good commentary though in many respects highly individual in its point of view.

*The Prophet of Reconstruction* by William Fredrick Lofthouse (London: Clarke). Not a commentary, but an account of Ezekiel's message from the older critical point of view.

*Daniel* by R. H. Charles. The New Century Bible.

*The Book of the Twelve Prophets* by George Adams Smith. The Expositors Bible (New York: Harpers. [1898] 1929). A still unsurpassed classic from an older generation.

*The Modern Message of the Minor Prophets* by Raymond Calkins (New York: Harpers. 1947). The most recent treatment of the subject. For the general reader.

*The Books of Joel and Amos* by Samuel Rolles Driver. Cambridge Bible for Schools and Colleges (New York: Macmillan).

*The Minor Prophets* by Samuel Rolles Driver. Nahum, Habakkuk, Zephaniah, Haggai, Zechariah, and Malachi. The New Century Bible.

*Meet Amos and Hosea* by Rolland Emerson Wolfe (New York: Harpers. 1945). An interesting, popular treatment. Includes some critical opinions of uncertain value.

*The Cross of Hosea* by Henry Wheeler Robinson (Philadelphia: Westminster Press). A brief and devout study of the prophet's personal tragedy.

### FICTION DEALING WITH OLD TESTAMENT CHARACTERS

*Joseph* by Thomas Mann (New York: Knopf. 1944). A massive and rewarding work for those who have the patience to read it. Not easy.

*David the King* by Gladys Schmitt (New York: Dial. 1946). Easy reading, very modern, not devout!

*The Giant Killer* by Elmer Holmes Davis (New York: The Readers' Club. 1943). Breezy and readable.

*The Herdsman* by Dorothy Clark Wilson (Philadelphia: Westminster. 1946). The career of Amos. Highly recommended.

*Hearken Unto the Voice* by Franz V. Werfel (New York: Viking. 1938). The life of Jeremiah. Easily the best novel on an Old Testament subject.

## THE PERIOD BETWEEN THE TESTAMENTS

### RELIGIOUS AND POLITICAL HISTORY

*Jerusalem Under the High Priests* by Edwyn Robert Bevan (New York: Longmans Green).

Environment, Social, Political, Intellectual, and Religious, of Israel from the Maccabees to our Lord by Edwyn Robert Bevan in Gore's *A New Commentary on Holy Scripture.*

*Religious Development Between the Old and New Testaments* by Robert Henry Charles (Home University Library. 1914).

*The Jews and Judaism During the Greek Period* by William Oscar Emil Oesterley (New York: Macmillan. 1941).

*Judaism in the Greek Period* by George Herbert Box (New York: Oxford. 1932). The Clarendon Bible, Vol. 5.

See also below under Religious and Cultural Background of the New Testament.

## INTRODUCTION TO THE APOCRYPHAL BOOKS

*The Apocrypha and Pseudepigrapha of the Old Testament* edited by Robert Henry Charles (New York: Oxford. 1913). The standard work for scholars. Two large volumes containing introduction, text, and commentary for all the books of the Old Testament Apocrypha and also for those books, never part of any Canon of Scripture, which are called Pseudepigrapha.

*A Source Book of Interbiblical History* by W. H. Davis and E. A. McDowell (Nashville: Boardman Press). Gives the actual text of the most important documentary material for the period 400 B.C. to 79 A.D.

*The Story of the Apocrypha* by Edgar Johnson Goodspeed (Chicago: University Press. 1939). Brief and readable.

*An Introduction to the Books of the Apocrypha* by William Oscar Emil Oesterley (New York: Macmillan. 1935).

*The Apocryphal Literature* by Charles Cutler Torrey (New Haven: Yale. 1945). Has the advantage of including the so-called pseudepigraphical books, but some of the critical views are highly individual.

*The History of New Testament Times,* with an Introduction to the Apocrypha by Robert Henry Pfeiffer (New York: Harpers). The latest treatment of the subject. The history is excellent, the Introduction somewhat technical.

THERE is no substitute for some firsthand acquaintance with actual contemporary documents. The most important religious books relating to the times are the so-called pseudepigrapha, especially I Enoch, IV Esdras, and II Baruch, which are included in Charles' mammoth *Apocrypha and Pseudepigrapha of the Old Testament* (New York: Oxford). These picture the strange world of "apocalyptic" which was so important in New Testament times. The second great strain of thought in the religious world of the Jews was that of rabbinical or normative Judaism. Some impression of this world, in all its vastness and complexity, can be gained by dipping into *The Mishnah,* translated by H. Danby (New York: Oxford), and *A Rabbinic Anthology,* a volume of selections from the haggadic or edifying literature of the Jews, edited by C. F. Montefiore and H. Loewe (London: Macmillan). Another variety of Jewish thought, although no one knows how widespread it really was, is the Hellenistic Judaism found in the writings of *Philo Judaeus* (Cambridge: Harvard. The Loeb Classical Library, 10 vols.), as well as in the apocryphal book of *Wisdom* and the pseudepigraphic IV Maccabees. The principal sources for the history of the times are the voluminous writings of Josephus, particularly *The Antiquities of the Jews* and *The Jewish War*. The best edition is that of the Loeb Classical Library (trans. by Thackeray and Marcus) in 9 vols. *The Jewish War* can also be obtained in a cheap edition in Everyman's Library (New York: Dutton).

The material relating to the Greek and Roman background of the Gospels is too vast even to be summarized here. The average reader will probably have to depend largely on secondary sources of information.

### INDIVIDUAL BOOKS OF THE APOCRYPHA

*II (IV) Esdras* by William Oscar Emil Oesterley. Westminster Commentaries.

*The Wisdom of Solomon* by John Allen Fitzgerald Gregg. Cambridge Bible for Schools and Colleges (New York: Macmillan).

*Ecclesiasticus* by William Oscar Emil Oesterley. Cambridge Bible for Schools and Colleges (New York: Macmillan).

*The First Book of Maccabees* by William Fairweather and J. S. Black. Cambridge Bible for Schools and Colleges (New York: Macmillan).

### NOVELS

*My Glorious Brothers* by Howard Melvin Fast (Boston: Little, Brown. 1948). The exciting story of the wars of the Maccabees.

## BOOKS ON THE NEW TESTAMENT

### THE RELIGIOUS AND CULTURAL BACKGROUND OF THE NEW TESTAMENT

*A History of the Jewish People in the Time of Jesus Christ* by Emil Schuerer (New York: Scribners). The classic work on the subject of the Jewish background. Too detailed for the ordinary reader and in its English edition considerably out of date.

*Judaism in the First Centuries of the Christian Era* by George Foot Moore (Cambridge: Harvard. 1927). Another classic; also very detailed. Interesting reading for those who have the time.

*Jew and Greek, Tutors to Christ* by Alexander Converse Purdy and George Hogarth C. MacGregor (New York: Scribners. 1936). The best book for the general reader on both the Jewish and pagan background of the Gospels.

*The Background of the Gospels* by William Fairweather (Edinburgh: Clark).

*The Pharisees* by Robert Travers Herford (New York: Macmillan. 1924).

*Judaism in the New Testament Period* by Robert Travers Herford (London: Lindsey).

*The Religion and Worship of the Synagogue* by William Oscar Emil Oesterley and G. H. Box (England: Pitman, Bath).

*The Relevance of Apocalyptic* by Harold Henry Rowley (London: Lutterworth Press. 1944).

### THE HELLENISTIC BACKGROUND OF CHRISTIANITY

*The World of the New Testament* by Terrot Reaveley Glover, New York: Macmillan. 1936).

*The Pagan Background of Early Christianity* by R. H. Halliday (University of Liverpool Press).

*Hellenistic Civilization* by W. W. Tarn (London: Arnold).

*The Environment of Early Christianity* by Samuel Angus (New York: Scribners. 1915).

*The Religious Quests of the Greco-Roman World* by Samuel Angus (New York: Scribners. 1929).

### POLITICAL AND ECONOMIC BACKGROUND OF JESUS' TEACHING

*Toward the Understanding of Jesus* by Vladimir Gregorievitch Simkhovitch (New York: Macmillan. [1927] 1937).

*The Economic Background of the Gospels* by Frederick Clifton Grant (New York: Oxford. 1926).

### THE HISTORY OF THE NEW TESTAMENT PERIOD

*A History of New Testament Times in Palestine* by S. Mathews (New York: Macmillan. 1910). A good brief survey of the historical background.

*New Testament History* by George Woosung Wade (New York: Dutton. 1922). Not only a history, but an encyclopedia of information about New Testament background. See also above *Introduction to the Apocryphal Books* under R. H. Pfeiffer.

IN addition to the books previously listed under Geography of the Bible (see page 194) special mention should be made of the delightful travel books of H. V. Morton, *In the Steps of the Master* and *In the Steps of St. Paul* (New York: Dodd, Mead).

### GENERAL SURVEY OF NEW TESTAMENT LITERATURE

*The Story of the New Testament* by Edgar Johnson Goodspeed (Chicago: University Press). Easy reading.

*New Testament Life and Literature* by Donald Wayne Riddle and H. H. Hutson (Chicago: University Press. 1946). Written from a purely secular and humanistic standpoint.

*The Beginning of Christianity* by Clarence Tucker Craig (Nashville: Abingdon-Cokesbury). A general survey of the history of Christianity in the apostolic age in which all the literature is discussed in its historical order. For the mature inquirer.

*Christian Beginnings* by Morton Scott Enslin (New York: Harpers. 1938). The history and the literature.

*The First Age of Christianity* by Ernest Findlay Scott (New York: Macmillan. 1926). Similar in purpose to the above, but much briefer. Good for a quick over-all view.

*The Making of the New Testament* by Benjamin Wisner Bacon (Home University Library. 1912). Rather technical for the ordinary reader.

### INTRODUCTION TO THE LITERATURE OF THE NEW TESTAMENT

*The Literature of the New Testament* by Ernest Findlay Scott (New York: Columbia. 1932). A standard and relatively conservative work.

*An Introduction to the Literature of the New Testament* by James Moffatt (New York: Scribners. 1911). Distinctly for the scholar. An old book but still useful.

*An Introduction to the New Testament* by Edgar Johnson Goodspeed (University of Chicago Press. 1937). Easy to use, but somewhat individualistic.

*The New Testament, Its Making and Meaning* by Albert Edward Barnett (Nashville: Abingdon-Cokesbury. 1946). The most recent treatment of the subject. Popular rather than original.

*An Introduction to the New Testament* by Kirsopp and Silva Lake (New York: Harpers). Scholarly but intended for popular use.

208

### HARMONIES OF THE GOSPELS

ANY serious student of the Synoptic Gospels will wish to have the material before him in such form that the different accounts can be easily compared. A satisfactory harmony arranges the Gospels in parallel columns.

*A Harmony of the Synoptic Gospels* by Ernest Dewitt Durton and E. J. Goodspeed (New York: Scribners. 1917).

*The Synoptic Gospels* by James Matthew Thompson (New York: Oxford).

*A Syllabus and Synopsis of the First Three Gospels* by Walter Ernest Bundy (Indianapolis: Dobbs-Merrill. 1932). Text of the American Standard Version.

*Gospel Parallels* (New York: Nelson. 1949). A synopsis of the first three Gospels using the text of the Revised Standard Version and produced under the supervision of the revision committee. Includes also non-canonical parallels.

### THE RELIGIOUS IDEAS OF THE NEW TESTAMENT

*The Theology of the New Testament* by George Barker Stevens (New York: Scribners. 1899). Old, but still useful. Primarily for the minister and scholar.

*The Religion of the New Testament* by Ernest William Parsons (New York: Harpers. 1939). Not, on the whole, a very satisfactory work, but one of the few available.

*The Varieties of New Testament Religion* by Ernest Findlay Scott (New York: Scribners. 1943). A useful book although emphasizing somewhat onesidedly the variety, as opposed to the unity, of New Testament thought.

*One Lord, One Faith* by Floyd Vivian Filson (Philadelphia: Westminster Press. 1943). A good antidote to the onesidedness of the above.

### THE LIFE OF JESUS

THERE is no satisfactory biography of Jesus and there never will be. The Gospels are not biographies in the conventional sense and do not provide the materials from which a biography can readily be constructed. Those who are interested in seeing how difficult it has proved to write the life of Jesus are recommended to dip into Albert Schweitzer's now classic *The Quest of the Historical Jesus* (New York: Macmillan) or C. C. McCown's *The Search for the Real*

209

*Jesus* (New York: Scribners). Ultimately every reader is thrown back upon the Gospels themselves and each must, within the broad framework of the Church's faith, write his own life of Christ. Nevertheless, stimulating insights will be found in all the following books, if one clearly understands that each of them represents only a partial and onesided view of a very complex subject.

*The Life of Jesus* by Maurice Goguel (New York: Macmillan. 1944). A scholarly, objective weighing of the evidence. For the specialist.

*Jesus of Nazareth* by Charles Gore (Home University Library. 1929). An honest attempt, by a noted scholar and Christian believer, to deal with the subject as objectively as possible.

*The Real Jesus* by Charles Fiske and B. S. Easton (New York: Harpers. 1929). Possibly the best single volume for the lay inquirer.

*A People's Life of Christ* by John Paterson Smyth (New York: Revell. 1934). A retelling of the Gospel story with no attempt to introduce critical points of view.

*The Short Story of Jesus* by Walter Lowrie (New York: Scribners. 1943). An interesting and original book, thoroughly critical in its approach to the subject, yet loyal to tradition and chiefly concerned with positive religious meanings.

*Jesus of Nazareth* by Joseph Klausner (New York: Macmillan. 1925). A life of Jesus by an eminent Jewish scholar, with all the limitations which that naturally imposes, but with a fascinating amount of useful background information.

*The Life of Jesus* by Conrad Noel (New York: Simon, Schuster. 1937). A popular and non-critical account, but emphasizing uniquely the social aspect of Jesus' teaching.

### THE TEACHING OF JESUS

This subject is, to some extent, also covered in the above mentioned lives of Jesus.

The Sayings of Jesus by Thomas Walter Manson (in Major, Manson and Wright, *The Mission and Message of Jesus*) (New York: Dutton. 1937).

*The Teaching of Jesus* by Thomas Walter Manson (Cambridge University Press. 1935). Much more technical than the above.

*The Teachings of Jesus* by Bennett Harvie Branscomb (Nashville: Abingdon-Cokesbury. 1931).

*The Religion of Jesus* by Walter Ernest Bundy (Indianapolis: Dobbs-Merrill. 1928).

*The Jesus of the Parables* by Charles F. W. Smith (Philadelphia: Westminster Press. 1948). Highly recommended.

*The Parables of the Synoptic Gospels* by Bertram Tom Dean Smith (Cambridge University Press. 1938).

*The Sermon on the Mount* by Martin Dibelius (New York: Scribners. 1940). A significant modern work. Somewhat individual in approach.

*The Ethical Teaching of Jesus* by Ernest Findlay Scott (New York: Macmillan. 1925). A readable brief discussion.

*The Religion of Maturity* by John Wick Bowman (Nashville: Abingdon-Cokesbury. 1948). An attempt to show how the religion which Jesus taught was the logical culmination of Old Testament thought.

*Jesus the Messiah* by William Manson (Philadelphia: Westminster Press. 1943). An examination of the self-consciousness of Jesus, His sense of messiahship.

*Christ in the Gospels* by Alfred Edward John Rawlinson (New York: Oxford. 1944).

### THE LIFE AND THOUGHT OF ST. PAUL

*Paul* by Arthur Darby Nock (Home University Library. 1938). The best brief book on Paul; inexpensive.

*St. Paul* by Wilfred Lawrence Knox (New York: Appleton. 1932). A very brief, yet scholarly sketch of Paul's life and religious development.

*Paul* by Edgar Johnson Goodspeed (Philadelphia: Winston. 1947). Popular and readable.

*St. Paul* by Gustav Adolf Deissmann (New York: Doran. 1927). Important and easy to read. A good corrective for the idea that Paul was primarily a systematic theologian.

*Paul for Everyone* by Chester Warren Quimby (New York: Macmillan. 1944). A popular sketch of both Paul's life and thought.

*A Man in Christ* by James Stuart Stewart (New York: Harpers. 1933). Probably the most satisfactory comprehensive account of the mind of Paul.

*Christianity According to St. Paul* by Charles Archibald Anderson-Scott (New York: Macmillan. 1927). Good, but less original than the above.

*Paul of Tarsus* by Terrot Reaveley Glover (New York: Harpers).
A valuable and scholarly collection of essays.

*The Apostolic Age* by Arthur Cushman McGiffert (New York: Scribners. o.p.). Old but still useful.

*Christian Beginnings* by Morton Scott Enslin (New York: Harpers. 1938). Solid, but readable; contains also a good history of New Testament times.

*The Nature of the Early Church* by Ernest Findlay Scott (New York: Scribners. 1942).

*The Beginnings of the Christian Church* by Hans Lietzmann (New York: Scribners. 1934).

*The Apostolic Preaching and Its Developments* by Charles Harold Dodd (London: Hodder and Stoughton. 1936). The faith which the early Church proclaimed.

COMMENTARIES ON INDIVIDUAL BOOKS OF THE NEW TESTAMENT

THE remarks made above (under The Old Testament) about the various series of commentaries on the books of the Bible hold also for those volumes which deal with the New Testament, except in the case of the Clarendon Bible which, in the New Testament field, is a series of commentaries on the separate books rather than a treatment of selected highlights. There is, however, for the New Testament a special series, *The Moffatt New Testament Commentary* (New York: Harpers) which is easily the best of all. These commentaries are thorough, yet non-technical, and all are of comparatively recent date. While there is naturally considerable variation in the quality of the individual volumes, yet all can be recommended to the educated inquirer. For the person who knows Greek and desires a more extensive commentary than the Moffatt series affords, there is an excellent series published by Macmillan which has been coming out over a period of many years and is not yet complete.

*The Mission and Message of Jesus* by H. D. A. Major, T. W. Manson, and C. J. Wright (New York: Dutton). A conveniently arranged one-volume commentary on all the Gospels. The different parts are of uneven value, Manson's contribution being much the best.

*The Gospel of Matthew* by Theodore Henry Robinson. Moffatt New Testament Commentaries (New York: Harpers. 1928).

*Saint Matthew* by Frederick Wastie Green. The Clarendon Bible (New York: Oxford. 1936).

*The Gospel of Mark* by Bennett Harvie Branscomb. Moffatt New Testament Commentaries (New York: Harpers. 1937).

*Saint Mark* by Alfred Walter Frank Blunt. The Clarendon Bible (New York: Oxford. 1929).

*The Earliest Gospel* by Frederick C. Grant (Nashville: Abingdon-Cokesbury. 1943). A collection of essays dealing with special problems.

*The Gospel of Luke* by William Manson. Moffatt New Testament Commentaries (New York: Harpers. 1930).

*St. Luke* by Henry Balmforth. The Clarendon Bible (New York: Oxford. 1930).

*The Gospel of John* by George Hogarth MacGregor. Moffatt New Testament Commentaries (New York: Harpers. 1929).

*The Fourth Gospel* by Sir Edwyn Clement Hoskyns and Francis Noel Davey (London: Faber and Faber. 1940). A profound and important work. For the theologian.

*Christianity According to St. John* by Wilbert Francis Howard (Philadelphia: Westminster Press. 1946). Essays on various aspects of Johannine thought.

*The Acts of the Apostles* by Frederick John Foakes-Jackson. Moffatt New Testament Commentaries (New York: Harpers. 1931).

*The Acts* by Alfred Walter Frank Blunt. The Clarendon Bible (New York: Oxford. 1934).

*The Epistle of Paul to the Romans* by Charles Harold Dodd. Moffatt New Testament Commentaries (New York: Harpers. 1932).

*Romans* by Kenneth Escott Kirk. The Clarendon Bible (New York: Oxford. 1937). The best volume in this series.

*Paul's Epistle to the Romans* by Ernest Findlay Scott (New York: Scribners. 1947). Brief and popular. All three of the above may be recommended highly. One should also mention here the old, but important, commentary in the International Critical Commentary series by W. Sanday and A. C. Headlam.

*The First Epistle of Paul to the Corinthians* by James Moffatt. Moffatt New Testament Commentaries (New York: Harpers. 1938).

*First Corinthians* by A. W. Robertson and A. Plummer. International Critical Commentary.

*The Second Epistle of Paul to the Corinthians* by Robert Harvey Strachan. Moffatt New Testament Commentaries (New York: Harpers. 1936).

*The Epistle of Paul to the Galatians* by George Simpson Duncan. Moffatt New Testament Commentaries (New York: Harpers. 1934).

*Thessalonians and Galatians* by Walter Frederic Adeney. The New Century Bible.

*The Epistles of Paul to the Colossians, to Philemon, and to the Ephesians* by Ernest Findlay Scott. Moffatt New Testament Commentaries (New York: Harpers. 1930).

*The Epistle of Paul to the Philippians* by John Hugh Michael. Moffatt New Testament Commentaries (New York: Harpers. 1929).

*Thessalonians and Galatians* by W. F. Adeney. The New Century Bible.

*Thessalonians* by J. E. Frame. International Critical Commentary.

*The Pastoral Epistles* by Ernest Findlay Scott. Moffatt New Testament Commentaries (New York: Harpers. 1937).

*The Pastoral Epistles* by Burton Scott Easton (New York: Scribners. 1947). Intended for the general reader.

*The Epistle to the Hebrews* by Theodore Henry Robinson. Moffatt New Testament Commentaries (New York: Harpers. 1933).

*The Epistle to the Hebrews* by Ernest Findlay Scott (New York: Scribners).

*The General Epistles, James, Peter, and Judas* by James Moffatt. Moffatt New Testament Commentaries (New York: Harpers. 1928).

*The First Epistle of Peter* by Edward Gordon Selwyn (New York: Morehouse-Gorham. 1941). The most recent addition to the Macmillan series. For the specialist.

*The Johannine Epistles* by C. H. Dodd. Moffatt New Testament Commentaries (New York: Harpers. 1946).

*The Book of Revelation* by Ernest Findlay Scott (New York: Scribners. 1940).

*The Revelation of John* by Shirley Jackson Case (University of Chicago Press. 1919).

*The Apocryphal New Testament* by Montague Rhodes James (New York: Oxford. 1924).

# Index

Babylonian Empire, 67, 68, 69, 83, 85, 89, 91
Babylonian Exile; *see* Exile, Babylonian
Balaam, 44
Baptism, 162–163
Barak, 46
Barnabas, St., 152, 154, 155
Bartholomew, St., 137
Baruch, 82
Bathsheba, 53, 54
*Benedictus,* 129
Berea, 155
Bethany, 143
Bethel, 38
Bethlehem, 50, 128
Bible, definition of, 5, 24; *see also* Devotional use of; Inspiration; Revelation; Unity; Word of God
Bildad, 94
Bishops, 165, 167

## C

Caesarea Philippi, 140, 156
Caiaphas, 145
Cain, 33
Canaan, 35; *see also* Conquest
Canaanites, 35, 36, 37, 44, 45, 46, 52, 65, 88
Carmel, Mt., 57
Catholic Church, 150, 155
Chaldeans, 68
Christ, 115, note, 127, 139–140; *see also* Jesus; Messiah
Chronicles, Books of, 45, 70, 93
Church, the body of Christ, 161, 163, 168, 175; the bride of Christ, 99, 162, 175; the new Israel, 8, 20, 119, 138, 141, 150, 152, 153, 162, 164, 166; life in, 159–169; communal living, 167–169; membership, 162–163; ministry, 166–167; worship, 163–166; spread of, 150–158
Circumcision, 35, 112
Colossians, Epistle to, 157, 175
Communion, Holy; *see* Lord's Supper

Conquest (of Canaan), 45–46
Corinth, 156, 166, 171
Corinthians, Epistles to, 147, 171–174
Covenant, with Abraham, 35; with Moses, 41; with Noah, 34; New, 84, 108, 136, 144, 161; Old Testament idea of, 105–108, 112
Creation, 30–33
Cyprus, 152
Cyrus, 69

## D

Damascus, 152
Daniel, 74, 77, 86–87, 93, 109, 116, 180
David, 14, 28, 47, 48, 50–53, 54, 56, 61, 67, 95, 115, 116, 128, 140, 143, 147
Deaconesses, 167
Deacons, 151, 167
Dead Sea, 131, 142
Deborah, 46
Delilah, 47
Derbe, 153, 155
Deutero-Isaiah; *see* Isaiah, Second
Deuteronomy, 45, 65 and note, 66, 71, 109
Devotional use of Bible, 23–24
*Diaspora,* 76, 153
*Dies Irae,* 91
Dispersion; *see Diaspora*
Doctrine, Biblical, 15, 16, 173
Doctrine of God; *see* God, doctrine of
Doctrine of Man; *see* Man, doctrine of
Domitian, 180

## E

Ecclesiastes, 55, 93, 98–99
Ecclesiasticus, 21
E Document, 29 and note, 71
Edom, 89
Egypt, 19, 39, 40, 41, 105, 108, 125, 129
Egypt, flight into, 125
Egyptians, 42, 67

of, 55, 93, 97, 99; Wisdom of, 21, 28, 55, 97
Son, God the, 23, 127, 128, 130, 131, 148, 149, 186
Son of Man, 116
Spirit, Holy, 11, 23, 24, 64, 76, 148, 151, 157, 159, 160
Stephen, St., 151, 154
Suffering Servant, 82, 115, 116, 140, 147
Synoptic Gospels, 122 and note, 123–126, 127, 139, 141 note, 142
Syria, 62, 75, 139; see also Antioch, Syrian
Syro-Ephraimite War, 62, 80

### T

Tabernacle, 43, 112, 113
Tekoa, 89
Temple, 95, 112, 113–114
Temple, Herod's, 129, 143
Temple, Second (Zerubbabel's), 70, 96, 113
Temple, Solomon's, 55, 68, 69, 91, 113
Ten Commandments, 45
Testament, 107; see also Covenant
Testament, New, 12–17, 21–23, 107, 117, 125, 148, 167, 117–182
Testament, Old, 8, 12–17, 17–20, 25–116, 165, 186
Theophilus, 125
Thessalonians, Epistle to, 176, 177
Thessalonica, 155, 176
Thomas, St., 137, 149
Timothy, St., 155, 176
Timothy, Epistles to, 167, 177
Tishri, 112
Titus, Epistle to, 177
Tobit, 21
Torah, 105; see also Law

Trinity, doctrine of, 103, 160
Troas, 155
Twelve Tribes, 38

### U

Unity of the Bible, 12–17
Unleavened Bread, Feast of, 112
Ur, 35
Uriah, 53

### V

Verbal Infallibility, 11
Virgin; see Mary, St., the Mother of Jesus
Visitation, 126

### W

Wanderings in the Wilderness, 43–45, 112
Wisdom, 97–98, 103
Wise Men from East, 125, 128; of Israel, 97–98
Witch of En-dor, 51
Word of God, 9–10, 11, 24, 66, 103, 149, 185–187
Writings, The, 27, 93

### Y

Yahweh, 29, 41, 101; see also Jehovah
Yom Kippur, 112

### Z

Zacharias, 129
Zechariah, 70, 92, 142
Zedekiah, 68
Zephaniah, 66, 91
Zerubbabel, 70, 96, 113
Zophar, 94